# The Computers in Business Blueprint

## Christopher Barnatt

**BLACKWELL**
*Business*

The right of Christopher Barnatt to be identified as author of this work has been asserted in accordance with the Copyright, Designs and Patents Act 1988.

First published 1994

Blackwell Publishers
108 Cowley Road
Oxford OX4 1JF
UK

238 Main Street
Cambridge, Massachusetts 02142
USA

*British Library Cataloguing in Publication Data*
A CIP catalogue record for this book is available from the British Library.

*Library of Congress Cataloging-in-Publication Data*

A CIP catalog record for this book is available from the Library of Congress.

ISBN 0–631–19303–0

Typeset in 11 on 13 pt Palatino by TecSet Ltd, Wallington, Surrey
Printed in Great Britain by T.J. Press (Padstow) Limited, Padstow, Cornwall

This book is printed on acid-free paper

To my parents

# Contents

## PART I   The personal computer

## PART II   Management and computer application

**x** *Contents*

# List of figures

# List of tables

# Preface

*Good morning computer. Have you made that reservation?*
*And is there anything interesting in my mail?*

To some people, the days in which we may converse with business technology in the above fashion are sadly distant. Others are horrified that computers have attained their current population level and have actually become resident upon their desks. Whatever attitude people choose to adopt, we can be certain that computers are here to stay. Some businesses are totally dependent upon them, and many others are fast moving towards reliance on information technology. Whether it will be a 'good' morning when desktop machines aspire to the level of personal assistant is debatable. That sunrise will come, however, and thus everyone in business or education must be aware of the concepts and techniques applicable in business computer application.

No book of this size can attempt to detail the entirety of the business computing arena. What is undertaken is an investigation of the key conceptual topics and factual areas most likely to impinge on users of business computing technology in the years ahead. A non-technical approach is adopted throughout, with no logic diagrams, hexadecimal mathematics or complex flowcharts to be encountered. While these items are omitted, many powerful concepts are explored, such as the 'downsizing' theme that spans the book. The reader is therefore encouraged not to ignore the general introductory chapter if a thorough comprehension of the more specific business topics covered in later parts is to be fully appreciated.

After the introductory chapter the book is subdivided into two sections. Part I details common personal computer software and hardware, as well as explaining computer networks and communications. It is included due to the widespread use of personal computers in the modern office, as information processing is increasingly distributed away from central mainframe systems.

Part II opens up analysis to consider the business computer environment. It explores information systems, issues pertaining to computer implementation, security concerns, and the near and potential futures for computer application in the business world. At the end of the book there is a range of *Lotus 1-2-3* spreadsheet tutorial exercises, from which both students and practitioners with access to a personal computer and this industry-standard package (or compatible software) can develop a basic level of competence. Also at the end of the book is a comprehensive glossary of business computer terminology providing a quick reference for the student, academic or practitioner caught out by a segment of computer-prose or a jargon-spouting computer maniac.

And so to the acknowledgements! For their comments on drafts of various chapters, much appreciated thanks to Simon Ashby, Jim Devlin, Pauline Wong, Steve Moore, Noel O'Sullivan, Sandra Mienczakowski and Ken Starkey. In addition to my fore-mentioned colleagues I would like to thank (or console!) Helen Leverton and Helen Whalley for also suffering my fraught, tired and largely egocentric meanderings over the past seven weeks. Finally, special thanks to my father for encouraging my interest in computers, and to Mark Daintree for nit-picking his way through the entire *Blueprint* in addition to countless other as yet 'undiscovered' tomes over the past eight years. Yes, we must be getting old.

Christopher Barnatt

# 1 Introduction

Computers are part of our lives. Like it or not, with microchips controlling appliances as diverse as toasters to photocopiers, video recorders to factory robots, nobody in the modern workplace can avoid contact with **information technology** (IT). Two attitudes, however, may be adopted. The first is that of the ostrich, sticking one's head in the sand and pretending that nothing has really changed, or at least that others will deal with the computer revolution leaving you quietly playing with pencil and slide-rule in the corner. More sensibly, of course, you can decide to push ahead of the crowd and find out what all the fuss is really about. What can computers actually do? And perhaps just as significantly, what are they incapable of? This book explores these issues, addressing the positive and negative implications of increased computer application in modern business.

Both business microcomputing and wider organizational concerns related to IT are explored herein, providing a broad overview of the subject area. Throughout the text, the overriding aim is simple: to distinguish what business computer users really need to know, and what it is safe for them to be ignorant of. For example, an office manager does not have to know how to program a computer from scratch, or understand the arrangement of circuitry within the machine. He or she should, however, be aware of issues such as the range of tasks that may now be assisted by computer, current computer-related legislation, and problems inherent in system implementation at both corporate and user levels. This *Blueprint* therefore seeks to provide a non-technical pathway through the ever-expanding domain of business computing, cutting through the plethora of technobabble spouted by bleary-eyed technofreaks married to their screens, in order to explain the key concepts and terminology that any clued-up manager needs be aware of in business today.

## Information processing tools

At a back-to-basics level, computers, like hammers or powerdrills, can be viewed simply as tools created by humans to assist in their endeavours. Whereas the latter are designed to assist in physical construction, computers are tools enabling the rapid capture, manipulation, storage, retrieval and communication of information. Computers cannot think or act for themselves, and any intelligence with which they may one day be endowed will inevitably be limited by logic and bestowed upon them by their human creators. Thus computers will never take over the business domain, just as power looms did not take over the textile industry during the industrial revolution. This said, both power looms in the late 1700s, and computers two centuries later, have had considerable impacts on the nature of the workplaces they have come to inhabit, and the tasks that people have come to perform within them. Computers should not be seen as a threat within the modern office, but equally their impact on its nature, both socially and technically, cannot be ignored.

What makes a computer distinct from most other tools is its capacity to be programmed. Whereas a hammer is dedicated solely to tasks requiring sudden powerful impulses on small areas, a computer can be programmed to perform a variety of useful functions. A modern personal computer is equally at home performing complex calculations, producing graphs, sorting company records, recording sound, playing games, drawing animation, or assisting a scatter-brained writer in the preparation of a legible and error-free text. Most computer **users**, of course, only utilize their machines for perhaps one or two **applications** (the **word processing** of documents being by far the most common example). It is important to appreciate that this is usually not due to limitations in the **hardware** a user possesses (i.e. the physical components of their system), but to the lack of **software** (or programs) necessary to put their machine to a greater variety of uses. In turn, the limited number of software applications employed by most users may well be due to their ignorance of the broader range of activities to which their computer hardware may be applied. Hence it becomes clear why computer software publishers, rather than hardware manufacturers, now dominate the computer industry; their objectives being tied to expanding the application horizons of users already endowed with hardware capable of executing new types of program.

## Hardware, software and data media

The distinction between physical computer hardware, and the more transient software that is required to put it to productive use, needs to be carefully understood. By definition, software is not physical in nature, although it is usually supplied on some sort of physical **data media**, such as a **floppy disk**. To analogize, audio compact disks are a physical data media (chunks of pressed silver plastic), containing information that the CD player in a hi-fi can decode into music for its owner's enjoyment and their neighbour's discontent. And as with the CD player, computer hardware is merely a useless conglomeration of electronics if no software is supplied to bring it into meaningful operation. What does distinguish computer hardware from CD equipment, is the fact that what is supplied on the computer's data media can be of two variants – either data (structured information) or programs (computer software).

Data is the raw material with which computer hardware and software work, and symbolically represents ideas, concepts and communication patterns of meaning to the computer user. For example, computer data may be used to represent numbers, text, images or sounds. Programs, on the other hand, consist of sets of instructions that specifically define the way in which the computer hardware will manipulate, store and output the data it receives. To the hardware, all data supplied appears the same (consisting at its most basic level of a near endless stream of numerical digits '1' and '0' in a form known as **binary code**). Different computer programs, however, will interpret data in different ways – a word processor manipulating the ream of numbers as text, an accounts program treating them as balances and formula, and so on. The power of the computer as a programmable tool is thus revealed. For whereas your audio CD player can only process its incoming data into musical output, computer hardware (under software manipulation) can process, store and communicate apparently indistinct data forms in an almost limitless variety of formats. Computers may therefore be viewed as data processing systems, as illustrated in figure 1.1.

## Data processing and computer classifications

The common representation of a computer as a four-component data system can be viewed at many levels. One way of entering into such

```
          ┌─────────────┐
          │ I N P U T   │
          └─────────────┘
                 ║
                 ⇓
┌─────────────────────┐         ┌─────────────────┐
│ P R O C E S S I N G │ ⟨═════⟩ │ S T O R A G E   │
└─────────────────────┘         └─────────────────┘
                 ║
                 ⇓
          ┌─────────────┐
          │ O U T P U T │
          └─────────────┘
```

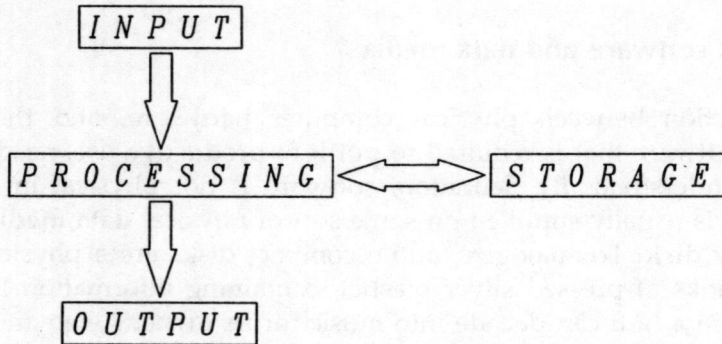

**Figure 1.1**   The computer: a data system

analysis is by distinguishing between four broad classifications of computer system, namely:

- the personal computer;
- the minicomputer;
- the mainframe; and
- the supercomputer.

## *The personal computer*

Personal computers (termed PCs) are the smallest classification of computer available. Also known as microcomputers, they offer a limited degree of processing power to a single user for a relatively low cost. Personal computers are therefore the kind of machine most likely to be encountered in the home or office, and are used for a wide range of applications from word processing to playing games. It is estimated that over 87 million personal computers have now been sold worldwide (Capron and Perron, 1993: 36), almost all of which have either been produced by IBM (International Business Machines), or are functionally compatible 'clones' of such IBM PCs.

To return to the example in figure 1.1, the input component of most personal computer systems will be a keyboard used by the user to input data, such as text into a word processed document. The processing subsystem may then be represented by the personal computer itself, usually housed within a box just under eighteen inches square and six inches high. Long-term storage, for example of word processed letters previously sent to clients, would most probably be upon one of several variants of floppy disk. Finally, output would initially be displayed on a television style monitor screen before being turned into **hardcopy** (final documents) on a desktop printer. This representation is, of course, highly simplistic, and a more detailed discussion of personal computer input and output hardware is entered into in chapter 3.

## *The minicomputer*

Next up from PCs, in terms of price and performance, come minicomputers. Although becoming less common in business, such machines are utilized where more data processing power than available via PCs is required. Depending on their application, minicomputers may be used by either single or multiple users. In the former case, the power of the machine is usually dedicated to one processing-intensive application, such as complex graphics modelling or design work. When minicomputers are used for image-intensive processing applications, they are sometimes referred to as graphics workstations.

Where minicomputers are used by many users simultaneously, their power processing is divided – e.g. between several users located in a particular office or building. Multiple user access to minicomputers is common for applications such as accounts processing in small or medium-sized firms, stock control, or for maintaining central record systems in relatively small organizations. Where multiple users are accessing the same computer system, they usually do so via **dumb terminals**. Such devices comprise a keyboard and display screen, and thus look similar to personal computers, although they have no native processing capacity. Terminal devices are thus totally reliant on their 'host' computer, being used simply for input and output, with processing for all users taking place centrally. Similarly, storage facilities for minicomputer systems are arranged on a central basis, rather than, for example, each individual user having access to their own floppy disk drive. Central storage facilities are clearly essential for accounts and other record-based data systems, as they allow many users to work upon the same data store, just as they would it they all shared a row of filing cabinets in the middle of a paper-cluttered, open-plan office.

Probably the most common minicomputer in business today is the AS/400, again produced by IBM. In other environments where minicomputers are utilized, such as universities and research establishments, the most frequently encountered machine is the VAX. Produced by DEC (Digital Equipment Corporation), this minicomputer is specifically targeted at user groups of scientists, academics and engineers.

Few would dispute that the days of the minicomputer are likely to be numbered. At one end of the market, the gap in processing capability between the PC and the minicomputer is rapidly decreasing, with PCs frequently offering more cost-effective computing solutions. At the other end of the spectrum, where perhaps very large data stores are required or many hundreds of users need access to the same computer system, more powerful mainframe computers are likely to be called into play. Both the price and performance divides between minicomputers and their larger mainframe cousins, however, are also diminishing, and indeed as technology advances the distinction between mini and mainframe computers is becoming increasingly blurred.

## The mainframe

Mainframes are very large computers used by a great many users, frequently across a wide range of locations. A large organization may have one mainframe computer based in its central headquarters, with users in regional offices, warehouses and even other countries having access to its facilities via dumb terminals. Input thus comes from a disparate range of sources, with outputs being similarly distributed. As with the mini-computer, processing and storage take place in a single location, although large corporations may operate many mainframe systems.

Banks and other financial institutions are one of the main user groups of large mainframe systems. All of a bank's branches and cashpoint machines are linked back to its mainframe computers. Thus, when an account holder inserts their sliver of plastic and personal code into the hole-in-the-wall to obtain some cash, they are actually initiating a flow of data processing and communication with their bank's central computer system. The output of processing a plea for cash will (usually!) be an instruction to the cashpoint hardware to dispense some paper currency, and in some cases to print a receipt. The system will also keep a record of the transaction in order that the customer's account balance may be altered in the central data store.

Records of required account changes in banking systems are accumulated throughout each working day. Such **batches** are then processed on the appropriate mainframe overnight, leading to the well-known one-day lag between cashpoint withdrawals and account balance changes. The reason for the operation of so-called 'batch systems' in banking is simple: there is far too great a demand on computer processing capacity in the day for interactive or realtime processing to occur. More generally, the lack of an instantaneous data processing capability is a characteristic of most mainframe systems. In some respects this is traditional, harking back to the early days of computing when input for processing was punched onto cards or paper tape before being run through the system. Ever since, mainframe computers have been optimized to process accumulated batches of input rather than to provide immediate user feedback. This does, of course, increasingly limit the extent to which management information systems can be totally based upon mainframe computers in the rapid-response-realm of modern international business.

## The supercomputer

For real power-users of computer hardware, to whom money is no object (usually because it has been purloined from others in the form of taxation), there is the supercomputer. Whereas PCs and minicomputers may process tens of millions of software instructions per second, and mainframes perhaps hundreds of millions, supercomputers can handle literally billions of calculations and data manipulations in less than the time taken to read this sentence. Indeed so quickly does processing take place that liquid nitrogen is circulated around the components of many supercomputers to stop them overheating. Their design is also frequently circular in nature so that information only has to flow down the shortest possible lengths of internal wiring.

Most computer users, of course, have no need for supercomputer power, even if they could afford the phenomenal price tags. A Cray-2 supercomputer, for example, currently retails at over $17m. Such prices have kept supercomputers the hardware of the power-hungry elite for many years, with the mighty machines mainly being used for military research, nuclear simulation and complex climate or geological system forecasting. The market for supercomputers, however, is now rapidly expanding, with super-hardware being applied to an ever-increasing range of applications. Most visibly in the public eye, motion-picture visual effects are now frequently supercomputer generated, as in box-office successes such as *Terminator 2* or *Batman Returns*. In the former, the title character was totally computer-generated (Jefferson, 1993), whilst in the latter, an entire army of penguins was modelled in 3-D by computer to be rendered to motion picture film stock.

Perhaps more significantly, supercomputers form the backbone of long-term research projects striving towards the conception of artificial intelligence (as discussed in chapter 8). If such projects are successful, and it becomes possible to construct super intellects within supercomputer data banks, the cost benefits of access to supercomputing hardware for corporate users will clearly increase. In turn, demand for such machines may rapidly expand in the non-too-distant future.

## The history of business computing

Having examined the basic nature of computers and their various classifications, we will take a brief step backwards to explore the conception, birth and adolescence of our now-common office companions. The evolutionary velocity of business computing has, by any standards, been staggering. In little more than thirty years we have witnessed the progression from machines crammed into large rooms, to personal computers leaving ample space on executive desks, and even hand-held devices that don't quite consume our jacket pockets. This text is being typed on a miniature computer more powerful than those used to send men to the moon, cheaper than a personal CD player, and which folds smaller than a domestic video tape. Indeed, with near perpetual transformation, computing has been: 'achieving technological leaps about once per decade comparable to the four-thousand-year path from horse and cart to bullet train' (Davidow and Malone, 1992: 76).

With such rampant progress, and the enormous technological chasm between modern computers and their recent ancestors in mind, anybody with an interest in the future of business computing is wise to have at least a cursory knowledge of the history of the fastest-growing industry of the twentieth century. For if the near-exponential developments in information technology, if only in terms of cost/performance ratios, are maintained as we approach the next millennia, the best (or worst) is surely yet to come.

### The generation game

Computer history is subdivided into generations, with present-day hardware and software debatably sitting somewhere between the fourth and fifth categorization of computer time. In fact, the exact boundaries between most generations may be contested. No specific dates are therefore assigned to the classifications that follow, being instead reserved only for specific events in history about which there may be no reasonable debate!

## The first generation

Although computational machines, such as the abacus, have existed for centuries, the first electronic computer was only constructed in 1945. Entitled ENIAC (Electronic Numerical Integrator And Computer), it weighed 30 tonnes, covered 15,000 square feet, was two storeys high, and programmed by 6000 simple on/off switches. Largely dedicated to atomic, meteorological and ballistics calculations, the unwieldy machine utilized 18,000 vacuum tubes. Such components, as well as being highly unreliable, produced a lot of heat and consumed tremendous power. Indeed, it has been reported that the lights of Philadelphia dimmed when ENIAC was turned on (Hanson, 1982).

Apart from its sheer size, and frequent downtime resulting from near-constant vacuum tube failure, ENIAC's major problem was that for each of the specific tasks to which it was applied, most of its 6000 switches had to be manually adjusted. Although even this limitation did not prevent ENIAC proving the viability of computers in certain computational areas (such as producing ballistics tables for the US army), it clearly constrained their wider application. As with many other major scientific hurdles, however, the problem proved to be conceptual rather than technical. Realising versatility would make or break computers, John von Neumann deduced that the machines, rather than relying on banks of on/off switches being set, could actually store their own programs. Von Neumann may thus be credited with the invention of computer software, in the form of simple programs – now termed operating systems – that instruct computers in the processing of incoming commands and information. Subsequently EDSAC (Electronic Delay Storage Automatic Calculator), the world's first stored-program computer, was built at Cambridge University in 1949.

As the 1950s dawned, the first commercial computers were constructed, still based on clumsy and space-consuming valve technology. UNIVAC (Universal Automatic Computer) was one such machine, based upon a mere 5000 vacuum tubes and performing around 1000 calculations per second. Sixteen UNIVACs were eventually built, three being used to process the 1951 US census – a task that would have taken longer than the decade span between returns without computer intervention.

Across the Atlantic, the United Kingdom was very much at the forefront of first-generation computer technology, though in an unlikely guise. Lyons, the giant food corporation, was the first British company to invest in computers. In 1953 it became the first organization to use computers for commercial data processing, building LEO (Lyons Electronic Office) to keep track of the payroll in its many teahouses of the era (Martin and Powell, 1992: 52–3).

## The second generation

The valve-based machines of the first generation indicated a potential role for computers in the business world. The future of computers in business was not secured until the mid 1950s, however, with the development of the transistor to replace unreliable vacuum tube devices. Pioneered in the Bell Labs, USA, transistors were smaller, cheaper, faster and more reliable switching devices than valves, and such desirable qualities were soon transferred to a new computer generation.

Aside from the birth of the transistor, the other major development of the second generation was the development of major computer programming languages. Such languages, most notably the scientific FORTRAN (FORmula TRANslator, 1954) and COBOL (COmmon Business Orientated Language, 1959), opened up computer programming to the less technically gifted. It thus became possible for business users to have their own dedicated applications (albeit by employing specialists in the new languages to write them). FORTRAN and COBOL thus overcame the log-jam in business computing development caused by a lack of people capable of actually programming the machines, and indeed were still widely used into the 1980s.

## The third generation

Whilst single transistors made computers smaller and cheaper, the development of integrated circuit technology in the 1960s, allowing their combination and miniaturization, made hardware smaller and cheaper still. Lithographic printing methods were developed allowing arrays of minute transistors to be etched onto silicon wafers, which were then encapsulated in plastic chips known as ICs (integrated circuits).

With IC technology developing, driven to some degree by the space-race of the mid-1960s, computer availability rocketed, and real mass-production of machines became possible. IBM launched its 360 series – a popular range of business mainframes made available in a variety of models according to user requirements. Developments in IC miniaturization continued apace, however, and indeed they have yet to come to a halt. So-called LSI (large scale integration) of components quickly gave way to VLSI (very large scale integration), and as consumer microelectronics became widespread a new generation of computers was born.

## The fourth generation

Whereas the first three computer generations were driven by large corporations and research institutions, it is interesting to reflect that some of the many fourth-generation developments sprang from the endeavours of small concerns and even wide-eyed enthusiasts. With the micro-processor chips that form the heart of all computers now available off-the-shelf, virtually anybody with a knowledge of electronics was free to construct their own computer. Jones and Wozniak are perhaps the most famous of such pioneers. In 1977 they created the Apple II, the original being housed in a rough wooden box! This machine sold in its tens of thousands, being the first *real* computer enthusiasts could own, and which business user could have on *their* desks. Key to the success of the Apple II in the business domain was the launch of the *VisiCalc* **spreadsheet** – a software package in effect offering users an electronic balance sheet. The Apple II with *VisiCalc* thus became popular with accountants, with spreadsheets still being probably the second most common computer software application (as detailed in chapter 2 and appendix I).

Radio Shack (known in the UK as Tandy) also launched a computer range at this time – the TRS80, introduced in 1978. The impact of these machines and those from Apple in the late 1970s and early 1980s is often forgotten – though by 1985 Apple and Tandy had shipped over 2 million personal computers.

In the early 1980s computers also entered the home *en masse* – pioneered to a large degree by Sir Clive Sinclair with his tiny ZX80 and ZX81 machines. Although possessing little processing power and without professional keyboards, these machines (which again sold in their millions) had three home-market strengths. Firstly, they plugged directly into domestic television sets, negating the need for an expensive monitor. Secondly, they included as standard the powerful fourth-generation language BASIC (Beginners' All-purpose Symbolic Instruction Code), so that users could write their own programs. Finally, they allowed data and programs to be stored and retrieved via domestic cassette recorders. Many, many teenagers and adults were infected with the computer-bug via Sinclair's early machines, even though they possessed little power and cassette recorder program storage was apt to be unreliable. What Sinclair was undoubtably successful at, however, was raising an awareness of what computers could be used for – many future business users being driven to investigate professional computing solutions from humble 'Sinclair beginnings'. Once again, as with von Neumann decades earlier, the barriers in computer application being addressed were conceptual.

With hindsight, the most significant development of the early 1980s, of course, was the launch of the IBM PC in the United States in 1981, and subsequently in the United Kingdom in 1983. Targeted specifically at business users, whilst other manufacturers' machines (such as those from Sinclair, Commodore, Atari and Texas) were concentrated on the home market, the IBM PC has come to dominate the computer world. IBM sold their product on grounds of reliability, ignoring price-competition, and providing excellent after-sales support. To business users such qualities, rather than technical innovation, were foremost in their system evaluations and almost certainly what gained IBM its initial market position.

IBM also allowed its IBM PC architecture to become 'open' – allowing other manufacturers to 'clone' their machines. This rapidly expanded the range of IBM PC compatible hardware in the business marketplace, in turn encouraging software publishers to concentrate on producing software for IBM PC machines. Nowadays it is almost certainly the vast software base available for IBM-compatible computers that maintains the IBM PC's dominant position within the industry. More software is available for IBM PCs than for any other computer, and new packages are being launched daily. It would have been most interesting if other computer hardware manufacturers in the early 1980s had allowed their systems to be open: the market potentially having developed in a very different pattern than that witnessed today. . .

Arguably computer technology and software development is still in the last throws of its fourth generation. A fifth generation, however, is commonly defined, wherein increasing hardware and software integration is making computers even more powerful, and increasingly accessible, for a wider range of users and applications.

## *The fifth generation*

Often credited to Japanese developments, the fifth generation of computer time tends to be characterized by more specific innovations those before it. It is commonly associated with developments pertaining to the following:

- artificial intelligence;
- expert systems;

- natural language computers;
- RISC and transputers; and (more generally)
- improved human–computer interaction (HCI).

The creation of a true artificial intelligence has long been the computer proponent's dream. The first few decades of computer development saw the progression from mighty, unreliable, valve-conglomerations to machines that could beat a man at chess. It therefore seemed extremely plausible that in years to come computers would be programmed with many facets of man's cognitive abilities and would take on unsavoury mental tasks. This, of course, has not been the case, and forms of general artificial intelligence are still many years away. Interestingly, it has been apparently 'simple' mental capabilities, such as language processing, that have proved most difficult to re-create in silicon hosts. Conversely, more 'complex' tasks, such as medical diagnosis, have been more straightforward to implant into mere machines.

The application of computers to narrow, strictly defined cognitive activities has lead to the creation of **expert systems**. Such software utilizes a vast data store, coupled with various complex rules (or heuristics) to solve problems in a specific field. Most common are expert systems developed for medical diagnosis, geological analysis, and tax or financial advise.

Also linked to the concept of artificial intelligence is the notion of natural language computers. Such machines would be programmed to respond to language as written or spoken in human conversation, rather than only to the explicit and syntactically complex commands as required by most existing machines. True natural language computers will therefore increase computer accessibility, especially for those who are not computer literate. As previously mentioned, however, language comprehension has proved extremely difficult to encode in software, and such computers are only likely to be part of a reasonably distant future.

On a more technical level, key developments of the fifth generation revolve around innovations concerning RISC and **transputers**. 'RISC' refers to reduced instruction set computers, indicating that these machines are based upon microprocessor chips with a very small range of internal operating instructions, which in turn allows them to operate at very high speed. The technicalities of RISC are somewhat complex (and the benefits also debatable), hence all the business user needs to aware of is that RISC-based machines are likely to run very, very quickly. In a similar vein, transputer developments refer to technological innovations whereby entire computer systems, rather than just components thereof, are etched upon single silicon chips. This negates the need for an array of different circuit components to be externally wired together, thus decreasing physical system size, increasing reliability, and making transputer-based machines much faster than conventional computers in operation.

Overall, the fifth generation of computers will not only be more powerful than their predecessors, but far easier to use – more *user friendly* – especially for technology-wary computer-phobics. In theory this will lead to greater computer application, not only at work, but also in the home. Whatever hardware and software developments take place towards this aim, however, the extent to which computers further encroach into human organizations and society will depend on the population's distrust or acceptance of newly emerging technologies. The fifth generation's success, more than any other, is therefore greatly dependent upon educating potential users as well as its key technological developments. The horse may quite easily be led to a silicon pool of technological marvels, but whether, and to what extent, it will drink is somewhat debatable.

## Current developments in business computer application

Having explored the nature of computers as data-processing systems, their variant classifications, and the developmental evolution of the computer industry, we may now turn our attention to key trends and concerns regarding modern computer application. Three significant developments will be isolated, to be utilized as recurrent themes throughout parts I and II of this *Blueprint*, and are the driving forces behind the structure of the book.

Specifically, current developments in business computing may be related to:

- The increased incidence of **downsizing**, leading to the more wide-spread application of personal computers (rather than mainframe-based systems).
- Improvements, and an ever-vigorous interest, in the *usability* of computer systems, sometimes at the expense of system end-power.
- Growing concerns regarding the hazards, for both users and organizations, of working with computer technology.

In short, the above point to a greater importance being placed on what type of computers are used in business, how they are used, and what drawbacks may result from such usage. In many ways, these interests have heightened as business computing, in terms of task-application, has approached a degree of maturity. In the booms of the profit-rich 1950s and

1960s, the concern was largely for businesses to *have* computer systems – to be seen to be investing in the latest technology, about which executives could ignorantly boast. Indeed, for several decades, computer and IT departments had virtually carte-blanche budgets, with near certain resource increases being allocated year-upon-year, and few questions ever being raised concerning efficiency and cost-effectiveness.

In the 1990s, however, the situation is very different. Alternatives to large mainframe systems exist, both technologically and in terms of market flexibilities. Disillusioned managers, fed up of being 'sandbagged' by computer experts 'looking for problems to solve' are increasingly 'applying return-on-investment accounting practices to computerization [asking] what will this do for our business?' (Mandell, 1991: 51).

Indeed, the cost-effectiveness of computer systems is now an issue high on the agenda of many organizations, whilst others are realizing that computers can be two-edged swords. In some companies, keen to concentrate resources on key activities, IT functions have simply been farmed out. Martinsons (1993) reports that as computing and telecommunications technologies have become increasingly difficult to manage, corporations keen on competitive advantage are outsourcing their IT-related risks and responsibilities. Eastman Kodak, Ford, General Motors, Metropolitan Life and Young & Rubicam are just some of best-known corporations turning-over their computer management to specialist concerns (Mandell, 1991; Martinsons, 1993), and others seem likely to follow the trend.

Even companies who deem outsourcing IT operations inappropriate now have pragmatic avenues for computer evaluation opening before them. Most commonly, the approach taken by organizations keen to restructure, but hesitant to outsource, has been the trend to downsize.

## The downsizing revolution

Probably the most important development in business computing in the past few years has been the rapidly increasing application of the microcomputer. Whereas ten years ago business computing was almost exclusively centred around large mainframes used jointly by many users, increasingly managers are running applications programs on personal computers within their own offices.

Information processing within the office environment is now increasingly 'distributed', with operations being carried out on many personal computers in multiple locations, rather than on central mainframe systems.

Accompanying and perhaps driving this trend towards increased microcomputer application has been the rise of reliable and cost-effective computer networks. With their personal computers connected to a network, many users, perhaps across a range of locations, are free to share both data and software packages. Networks of personal computers, rather than a host of dumb terminals connected to a mainframe, afford business users the flexibility of being able to run their own dedicated software (perhaps tailored to unique task specifications), whilst retaining the ability to access central data stores (such as stock level records or accounts data), as previously only possible via mainframe/terminal links.

This, to some alarming, move towards the increased utilization of a range of smaller computers in place of single mainframes, is most commonly referred to as 'downsizing'. Dan Trimmer, for example, a radical exponent of the cause, defines downsizing as: 'the comprehensive replacement of mainframe functions by cheaper – and possibly smaller and distributed – types of machine, for both existing and new applications' (Trimmer, 1993: 9).

The trend to downsize, as well as being driven by hardware developments, may also be attributed to increasing cynicism by managers regarding both the cost and complexity of their IT departments. By downsizing their computer systems away from often high-cost, bureau-cratic, mainframe-based support departments, mangers become free to control, develop and implement their own applications. Clearly this will lead to hostility from IT employees towards downsizing measures, if only due to concerns regarding their status and job security.

Education has a major role to play in downsizing's success, with many business computer users – including numerous IT specialists – being unaware of what is now technically feasible with small computers such as IBM PCs. With the broad advances in personal computer hardware, software, and significantly user maturity in the early 1990s, however, it is becoming increasingly apparent 'that a major threshold has been crossed, such that many large organizations over time will be able to dispense with mainframe computing entirely' (Trimmer, 1993: 3).

As well as allowing faster and more flexible system development, with users free to implement and adapt their own systems, downsizing also offers significant cost advantages. Firstly, there may be savings in staff costs, most notably in the IT department itself, which will almost inevitably contract in size as small machines proliferate. Secondly, the move towards the utilization of small computers attracts the advantage of significantly lower hardware costs, both in terms of initial capital outlay, and subsequent maintenance expenditure. Software will probably also be far cheaper for small machines in comparison to closed-architecture mainframe or minicomputer systems, with tried-and-tested PC business packages available off-the-shelf. The open-architecture of small computer systems also leads to more competitive hardware and software supply markets, offering computer users a wider choice of products and suppliers, and decreased risks of being lumbered with an unsupported system in the future.

The final downsizing advantages stem from actually having abundant PCs on users' desks throughout the office. As well as bestowing the ability to run new applications such as electronic mail systems, the physical proximity of PCs tends to foster a sense of proprietorship. Most employees become motivated to increase their own level of computer literacy when presented with their *own* PC, for whilst many new users 'may feel some trepidation, they may also be flattered by the trust placed in them and will typically look forward to their new roles as computer-literate beings' (Trimmer, 1993: 53).

As usual there is a flip-side to the coin, for although the move towards downsizing may lower costs and increase both user flexibility and motivation, the control that could once be wielded over company systems is likely to be greatly diminished. With mainframe-based systems, all software applications available to users on their terminals were created and maintained 'by the book' by programmers and systems analysts within the central IT department. With PCs on their desks, however, users capable of designing and adapting their own applications will probably enter into development in a fairly ad-hoc fashion. It is therefore conceivable that with corporate computer power widely distributed, overall efficiency may decrease due to the duplication of systems by different users unaware of the activities of others. More significantly, programs and data stores that are totally incompatible may be created by different users, thereby hindering efficient information transfer and communication. Finally, as end users move between jobs or companies, knowledge of their home-tailored applications will be lost, leading to time being wasted re-creating systems from scratch, or attempting to fathom their operations.

The trend towards downsizing thus has significant positive and negative implications for the modern business, and is the central reason why part I of this book is dedicated to PC hardware, software, networks and communications. The downsizing revolution does appear, however, to be rapidly gathering momentum – the monolithic mainframes of past decades are now seriously under threat from the upstart PCs of a new generation. Mainframes will, of course, maintain their usefulness in some areas of business (e.g. in banking, as in the previous cashpoint example), although the advantages of small computer systems are likely to continue to increase. This scenario would seem to suggest that the end-user computerization of the work environment is likely to continue over the years ahead, with fewer and fewer employees being able to avoid dependence on computer information systems. As with any major transitionary evolution bringing supposed advantages, there are significant problems associated with the increased utilization of computers in the workplace to bear in mind.

## Usability and computer systems

'Usability', apart from being one of those semantically uncouth words most people would be afraid to be caught with in public, is a term high on the agenda of most computer software publishers and hardware manufacturers. Whereas in previous decades people tended to be satisfied, or even amazed, when computers actually worked at all, nowadays usability is recognized as a critical factor in system evaluation. The discipline of human–computer interaction (HCI) is charged with addressing the usability of computer systems. It studies the work tasks to which computers are put, the wider work environment, and users' cognitive expectations and experiences in interacting with computer systems. Critically important for systems that are not only to be functional, but also safe, efficient, easy and enjoyable to use, is the nature of their **user interface**. To quote Preece:

> The user interface of a computer system is the medium through which a user communicates with the computer. The form of this interface has a strong influence on how the user views and understands the functionality of a system. Consequently, the user interface can be thought of as those aspects of the system with which the user comes into contact both physically and cognitively. (Preece, 1993: 13)

Two main variants of user interface may be isolated across most computer systems: command line and graphical. **Command line interfaces** (CLIs) require users to operate their computers by entering syntactically exacting lines of commands via the keyboard. Mistakes in entries are rarely tolerated, and hence CLIs alienate many potential users. For example in MS-DOS[(R)], the CLI on most PCs, to copy some information from one floppy disk to another the user would have to type in a command similar to the following:

COPY A:\DOCS\LETTER.TXT B:\DOCS

Although the nature of such commands is clear to programmers and hardened computer junkies, it hardly makes systems appear friendly to the majority. To overcome such difficulties, **graphical user interfaces** (GUIs) have been created. These represent applications programs and information files by small pictures (known as **icons**) on the computer screen so that users can more readily relate to them. These icons are then highlighted and/or moved around the screen to accomplish tasks, negating the need for users to remember exacting keyboard instructions. Document files will actually look like small pieces of paper, with floppy disks perhaps being represented by filing cabinets and drawers within them. To copy files between two disks, a user need only highlight the required document icon and move it to the desired new location. Graphical user interfaces hence make it easier for users to breakdown (or decompose) computer operations into meaningful subtasks, and permit a more coherent understanding of the system (Preece, 1993: 14). The most common GUI for the IBM PC is entitled *Microsoft*® *Windows*™, that along with the MS-DOS command line interface is discussed in greater depth in chapter 2.

It is worth noting at this point that although GUIs are far easier for users to relate to, they consume a far greater amount of processing power than their more daunting command line predecessors. There is thus an inevitable trade-off in terms of usability versus final system power when graphical interfaces are called into play. This has not, however, dissuaded most users from switching from CLIs to GUIs. It therefore appears that many people place usability higher on their list of priorities than, for example, operational speed. Either that, or users exploit the move to GUIs as an excuse to upgrade to more powerful (and more expensive!) computer hardware.

## *Employee health and corporate vulnerability*

The impact of computers on employee health and organizational vulnerability has only recently become a significant concern for most companies. With regard to the health of employees charged with working with computer equipment, many potential hazards have been identified, some of which are now being taken very seriously. Most long-term users of equipment comprising a keyboard and computer monitor (a **visual display unit**, or VDU) complain of either back and joint pains, eye strain and/or headaches. The effect of VDU radiation emissions upon users' eyesight (in the form of inducing myopia and increasing the risk of cataracts) is still being researched, as is the effect of such emissions on the health of foetuses.

**Repetitive strain injury** (RSI) in wrist, elbow and finger joints, resulting from intensive keyboard operations, is now recognized as a major potential health hazard of computer usage. In the 1990s more and more employees are complaining to their employers about RSI, with an increasing number suing for (and obtaining) large RSI-related compensation awards (Wood, 1992: 105). Companies are thus being forced to review the ergonomics of the computerized workplaces they have created for their VDU users, addressing factors such as lighting, seating, screen quality and rest breaks. The European Community is also taking a strong interest in this field: Directive 90/270/EEC came into force in January 1993 to promote employee safety and comfort in the use of VDU and related office equipment. Viewed at almost any level, the arena of computer-related ergonomics is rapidly gathering a high profile, and a more detailed evaluation is entered into in chapter 6.

For the organization, as well as its employees, computers may bring with them causes for concern. Most notably, vulnerabilities arise in corporate security as computerization becomes more widespread: 'The only phenomena that has grown faster than desktop computing is corporate vulnerability . . . [with managers] . . . overburdened, underbudgeted and often equally unaware of the real security issues' (Weiss, 1992: 447).

For example, whilst most people would never dream of leaving a confidential file lying open on their desk over lunch, many computer users will happily leave easy-to-copy floppy disks containing critical files lying idly around. Worse still, users may leave machines unattended whilst connected to sensitive information networks, or perhaps even write the passwords necessary to gain entry to such systems on notes attached to their VDU screens! Education has a major role in play in understanding the dilemma created by moves intended to facilitate greater access to computer systems, but which in doing so expose significant security concerns. The downsizing trend in particular creates major headaches, with desktop machines no longer enjoying the locational security previously assured to mainframe systems locked away in central locations. The increasing use of portable computers adds further to the problem – demonstrated most worryingly by the theft of a portable computer containing defence strategies from the boot of a car during the Gulf War in 1991. Due in no small part to the fact that all managers should be aware of the vast range of security threats related to computer usage, chapter 7 is dedicated to a detailed exploration of this notable area of corporate concern.

## Summary

This introductory chapter has reviewed the nature of computer systems. Computer history and classifications and have been explored, together with three key trends relating to the application of computers in business both at present and in the future. Specifically, chapter 1 has:

- Introduced computers as programmable data-processing tools comprised of both hardware and software.
- Distinguished between personal, mini, mainframe and supercomputers.
- Reviewed milestones in the history of computing across its five generations.
- Highlighted key developments in business computing concerning: (i) The trend towards 'downsizing', and thus the increasing importance of a knowledge of microcomputer application. (ii) The increasing emphasis on usability, with HCI developments such as the move towards utilizing GUIs. (iii) The increasing prominence of computer-related occupation health and corporate security concerns.

Subsequent chapters aim to flesh out specific detail over the skeleton so far described, providing both the microcomputer software and hardware knowledge so vital in modern business in part I, and exploring the wider environment of business computing in part II.

Finally, it is perhaps comforting to reflect on the fact that the science and philosophy of the computing domain is now so vast, and expanding so rapidly, that nobody can possibly seek to know everything there is to know about our electronic marvels of the twentieth century. What therefore becomes important, especially for those engaged in cut-throat, sink-or-swim business survival, is knowing a little more about computers than the jerk sitting next to you.

## Review and discussion questions

1. Why, more than ever, are personal computer skills important to managers who may have previously viewed small machines as simply tools for their clerical and support staff?
2. How have you personally come into contact with computers in both your work environment and daily life? Which of these impacts have been positive and which have been negative?

# PART I

# The personal computer

# 2 Personal computer software

This chapter concentrates on the personal computer software most commonly encountered in business today. To some it may seem strange that this book addresses business software before exploring the hardware on which it is run. It is a knowledge of the former rather than the latter, however, that most users first require in understanding business computer applications. For although hardware and software go hand-in-hand (the output of a desktop publishing program, for example, clearly being dependent on the printer hardware available), it is most frequently software (and a knowledge thereof) that governs the tasks to which computers may be applied. In other words, computer hardware exists to serve computer software, and not the other way around.

A knowledge of the range of software applications available should thus be the foremost weapon in the cerebral toolkit of anybody wishing to apply computer solutions to work applications. Indeed, without a knowledge of the type of applications programs they may wish to run, users will be incapable of specifying the hardware they require. Software-ignorant managers will at best be at the mercy of over-zealous salespersons when engaged in hardware purchase. At worst, they may find themselves signing purchase orders forwarded by technological magpies attempting to acquire every item of kit listed in the advertisements of their latest computer glossy.

## Off-the-shelf solutions

The majority of business microcomputing applications rely on the use of standard, off-the-shelf software packages. Supplied by mighty publishing corporations such as Microsoft, WordPerfect, Lotus and Borland, most business packages today are of a very high-quality (having progressed through a great many release versions), and can be tailored to the majority of tasks likely to be encountered within the office environment. Adopting such packages frees the business user from having to acquire a knowledge of computer programming, or the technicalities of how data is stored and processed within their machine. All such matters are taken care of by the software packages themselves, meaning that users need only become familiar with the general concepts and capabilities of standard packages in order to be well-armed to apply PCs to a vast range of productive activities.

The decision to utilize off-the-shelf packages may also free managers from the clutches of IT departments, to whom program development rather than completion is the major pleasure, and who invariably seem incapable of supplying tailor-programmed applications in increments of less than the obligatory man-year.

## Conceptual understanding

It should be noted at the outset that this chapter does not aim to provide a guide to the operation of specific software packages. There is no 'press key X to perform operation Y' analysis. The reasons for this are twofold. Firstly, there are far too many programs available within each business software category, each operating with slightly different commands and keystrokes, to list all potential operational specifics. Secondly, having evolved through continuous upgrades, most popular programs exist in a great many versions which themselves are not 100 per cent syntactically identical in operation. Any attempt at a 'global manual' approach is therefore futile.

Fortunately, the principles behind all programs in each applications category are the same. Thus once you understand what a particular type of software application does and why, it is a fairly straightforward task to learn the procedures required to operate an individual program. (This said, appendix I does provide hands-on exercises for those taking their first steps in the operation of so called 'spreadsheet' packages.)

## Operating systems and applications packages

Before our voyage through the different classifications of business software commences, we must distinguish between two software variants: **operating systems** and **applications packages**. The latter are the programs (like word processors and spreadsheets) employed for specific business activities, such as report writing and financial forecasting. Also known as 'high-level' programs, applications packages are utilized for productive work within the office. Equally important, though frequently forgotten, however, are the lower-level 'operating system' programs that assist both ourselves and our applications software in trouble-free operation.

## *What is an operating system?*

A computer's operating system serves as the intermediary between the computer's hardware at its most basic level, and the high-level programs employed by most users. Many people are ignorant of even the existence of their computer's operating system. It is, however, a vital software component, charged with controlling devices such as disk drives for data storage, as well as allocating memory to applications programs, and coordinating input and output hardware such as the keyboard and the printer. In their own attempt to explain an operating system's nature, IBM once described such programs as 'policemen' controlling the flow of information within computers and directing the traffic at busy intersections! (IBM, 1987: 1–4)

The operating system used with IBM and compatible PCs is known as **DOS** (Disk Operating System), sometimes prefixed as PC-DOS, or more commonly **MS-DOS**®, indicating that it was created by the software giant Microsoft®. Although currently in version 6, MS-DOS is still by many standards a rather archaic, low-level program. It utilizes a CLI whereby users must type exacting instructions in order to control file operations, and which many people find confusing. During their daily PC encounters most computer users avoid using DOS altogether. This is a pity, for although rather unfriendly, DOS does offer some reasonably powerful (if not essential!) tools for the task of **file management**.

## *MS-DOS and file management*

File management refers to operations performed in order to keep the information stored within a computer system tidy and clearly organized. It is thus totally analogous to the management of paper files in stuffed-full four-drawer cabinets. Both computers and manual filing systems soon deteriorate into chaos without somebody either imposing a strict regime on their operation, or at least taking them to task for a metaphorical spring-clean once in a blue or similarly tinted moon.

Computer programs and data files are usually stored on disk drive devices. These come in two basic forms – removable **floppy disks**, and the in-situ **hard disks** resident in all modern PCs. Floppy disks are normally used for the storage of computer data, and as the data media on which applications programs are supplied. Hard disks, in addition to storing user data files, also contain the computer's operating system and applications packages. The nature of floppy disks, and their higher-capacity hard disk cousins, is discussed together with alternative data storage devices in the next chapter.

Before being used to store data, all disks must be **formatted** – a process that initiates tracks and data *segments* on their media surface. In their unformatted state, disks may be analogized to empty libraries, potentially capable of holding books, but without the shelves necessary to accommodate published tomes. After formatting, a disk is like a library fitted out with shelves and an in-situ reference system – all prepared for data files to be stored and subsequently retrieved in a coherent fashion. The formatting of blank disks so that they may be used for data storage is therefore an essential function of DOS, and is carried out, not surprisingly, via a command known as FORMAT.

## Directories and subdirectories

Even when disks have been formatted, further file management is usually essential for their efficient operation. Just as libraries are divided into sections for ease of use (such as romance, thrillers, science-fiction and so forth), computer disks are usually divided into a range of distinct **directories**. A directory may be thought of as one of the drawers in a filing cabinet. A user, therefore, may use DOS to create one disk directory to store their document files, another in which to place accounts data, and a third to contain graphics images. Different applications packages will also be placed in their own directories on a PC's hard disk. Subdivision does not end here, however, with most disk directories further containing their own **subdirectories**. A user's DOCUMENT directory, for example, may be split into different subdirectories such as LETTERS, REPORTS and QUOTES.

DOS thus allows users to build up **directory trees**, with subdirectories existing within other directories and so forth, in an attempt to keep their ever-mounting computer data effectively organized. Most applications packages also utilize subdirectories to keep track of different aspects of the software and its associated data files. A word processor program, for example, may exist within a main disk directory entitled WP, with subdirectories entitled FONTS, GRAPHICS and SPELL used to store different typefaces, pictures and dictionary files. The MD (Make Directory), RD (Remove Directory) and CD (Change Directory) commands within MS-DOS are used to create, remove and navigate between different directories within a disk. Other common commands, such as DIR, COPY and ERASE are utilized in order to list the files within a particular directory, move files between different disks and directories, and to delete surplus files as required. A typical MS-DOS directory listing is illustrated in figure 2.1, this screen being representative of that glimpsed when glancing over the shoulder of a DOS-literate colleague engaged in low-level computer instruction. Note that there are four files indicated within this listing (TEST, TABLES, HELLO and POEM), together with one directory (<DIR>) entitled GRAPHICS.

The above, of necessity, has only begun to scratch the surface of the conceptual nature of MS-DOS. It has probably been sufficient, however, to put many readers off delving further into such matters! Fortunately for them, and due in part to the unfriendly nature of DOS, a more user-

```
A:\>DIR

 Volume in drive A is CJB-DISK
 Volume Serial Number is 3016-12E3
 Directory of A:\

GRAPHICS     <DIR>        07/05/93    12:24
TEST         WK1    1530  13/05/93    09:18
TABLES       WK1    4885  13/05/93    09:23
HELLO        DOC    1224  15/09/93    10:31
POEM         DOC    1238  17/10/93    23:11

        5 file(s)         8877 bytes
                        785143 bytes free
```

**Figure 2.1**   A directory listing in MS-DOS

sympathetic interface for file management and associated operations has recently been developed. Entitled *Microsoft*® '*Windows*™, this graphical environment is now available in version 3.1. An exceptionally popular software product, over 25 million *Windows* licenses have been sold since its launch in the late 1980s (*Computer Shopper*, 1993: 292), and indeed most hardware manufacturers now bundle *Windows* with their new PCs.

## *Windows: the graphical alternative*

Technically, *Windows* is not an operating system. It is instead a 'shell' run 'over' MS-DOS to protect users from the latter's unsociable disposition. A new version of *Windows* is currently in development, however, that will comprise a full operating system, independent of the presence of DOS on a user's hard disk to perform its functions. Entitled *Microsoft*® *Windows NT*™, its launch will almost certainly herald the death-knell of MS-DOS on personal computers within the office. At the time of writing, pre-release versions of *Windows NT* have already been supplied to applications program developers in their tens of thousands, and its release to the world at large is expected to be imminent.

*Windows* is often referred to as a **WIMP environment**, standing for Windows, Icons, Menus and Pointers. Applications programs and disk directories thus appear within their own 'windows' on the computer screen, which may be moved around and resized as the user desires. Icons (or little pictures) are displayed to represent applications programs and data files. To activate a program a user only needs to move their pointer (usually a little arrow) across the screen and subsequently 'click' on the required icon. Similarly, to copy a file between two locations, they only have to highlight the appropriate icon and drag it from one window to another. Pointer movements and clicks within *Windows* are usually achieved via an item of hardware known as the **mouse** – a small device with two or three switches whose movement on a flat surface in turn moves the pointer on the computer screen.

Finally, the *Windows* system allows command tasks (such as disk formatting) to be carried out from on-screen Menus. These are again pointer activated – most menus are selected by clicking on a menu bar at the top of the screen, causing a list of options to appear. The user can then use the pointer to highlight the option required, negating the need for exacting command line syntax to be remembered, as under the DOS system. Most users find that they become familiar with the *Windows* environment very quickly, although it does run more slowly than the DOS

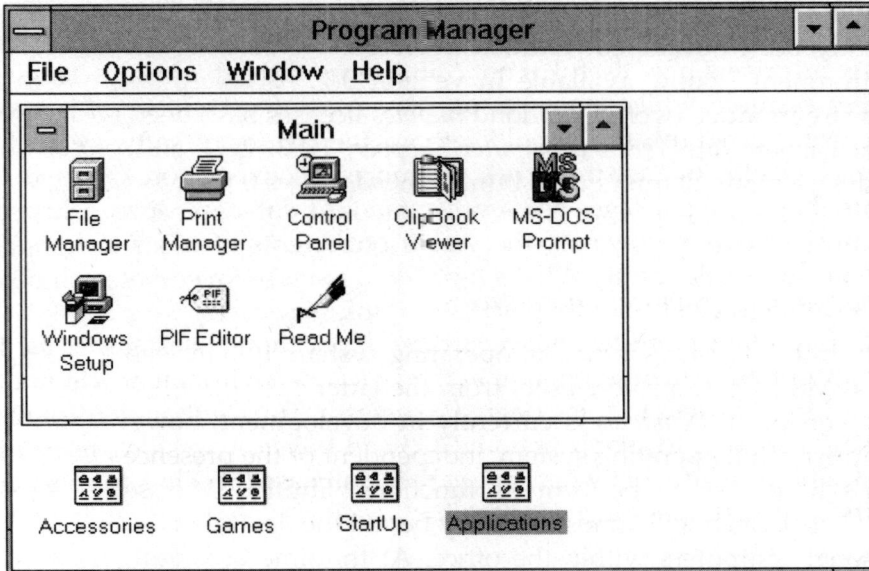

**Figure 2.2** Working in Microsoft® Windows™
Screenshot© 1985-1992 Microsoft Corporation. All rights reserved. Reprinted with permission from Microsoft Corporation.

CLI. The speed/usability trade-off between *Windows* and MS-DOS is particularly acute on older PCs, on which the *Windows* environment may run very slowly, if at all.

A typical *Microsoft® Windows 3.1*™ screenshot is provided in figure 2.2, illustrating a range of icons within rectangular windows, along with a menu bar at the top of the screen. A brief comparison with the previous DOS screen display (figure 2.1) clearly highlights the more aesthetic, user-friendly nature of *Windows* compared to MS-DOS. Finally, *Windows* is known to win early favour with many of its ex-DOS converts due to the fact that an excellent computer version of the card game 'Patience' is included free when *Windows* is supplied!

## Business applications packages

Having availed ourselves of a knowledge of the 'hidden' software on which we are so reliant, we can progress to consider the most common higher-level software applications encountered in modern business. Although specific package operations are not detailed herein, the best-selling programs in each software category are listed in order that the reader may become familiar with at least the names of the market leaders.

It is surprising how useful, if not comforting, such a basic knowledge can be. For example, whilst many people may guess that *WordPerfect* is a word processing program, few would fathom the nature of software such as *Paradox*, *Quattro* or *Sage* from their utterance in conversation. Once you are aware that these packages are simply standard database, spreadsheet and accounts software, however, the verbal onslaughts of office technophiles become far less daunting. What's more, you may discover that such people are less enlightened than they actually think they are!

An important point to note regarding applications packages is the fact that programs written to operate in the *Windows* environment will not run under MS-DOS, and to some degree vice-versa. Thus, although most major packages are now available in both DOS and *Windows* versions, users must be careful to ensure that when software is purchased it is in a form suitable for their chosen operating interface.

## Word processor software

By far the most common application for which personal computers are adopted is word processing, allowing PCs to be utilized in the creation, alteration and storage of written information. Gone are the days when mountains of paper were scrawled on in pen and ink, or viciously attacked via the cast-metal characters of the typewriter. Computers are much more efficient – whole rainforests of beautifully formatted output are spewed from a myriad of printers on a daily basis. As anybody who works in a PC-inhabited environment will tell you, the paperless office is a myth.

### The market players

There are a great many word processor packages available for IBM PCs, most of which offer the user an extensive range of facilities. Included in the plethora of common packages are:

- *WordPerfect*[TM];
- *Microsoft*® Word;
- *Lotus Ami Pro*[TM];
- *Multimate*[TM];
- *Protext*[TM]; and
- *WordStar*[TM].

*Word processor functions*

At a basic level, word processor programs turn computer screens into electronic pieces of paper. They thereby permit computer hardware to be employed as an electronic medium in which prose may be created, as well as allowing for the subsequent correction, development and alignment of written output before its commitment to paper. This genre of software can also perform complex manipulations on a user's precious text. The label 'processor' rather than 'word' should therefore remain paramount in a user's mind when learning to experience this frequently under-utilized category of computer software.

One of the most important features that immediately separates word processors from manual typewriters in entitled **word wrapping**. This refers to the process whereby text can be continuously typed into a word processor without the user having to press the carriage return key at the end of each line. Further, words that would become split at line-ends are automatically 'wrapped' down to the next. For example, if the following were typed into a word processor:

```
This is an example of a sentence being typed to demons
trate word wrapping
```

the word 'demonstrate' would not be cut between lines as above, but would wrap to the next, the screen displaying:

```
This is an example of a sentence being typed to
demonstrate word wrapping
```

This simple function is clearly incredibly useful, freeing the writer from a continuous wrestling match with line length, or the frequent inclusion of undue hyphenation. An additional function associated with word wrapping is termed **justification**. This refers to the method used to align the document's text between its margins. Various justification forms are illustrated in figure 2.3.

*Page breaks and document layout*

In addition to automating word wrapping and justification, word processors take control of the layout of text across a document's pages. Thus, when the text entered flows over a page in length, another is automatically begun. In effect, word processors offer a infinitely long scroll on which to type, dividing their user's input into 'real' pages at the printout

---

This is an example of left justification.  The text is aligned to the left-hand margin only.  Some people think left justification looks informal and friendly.

This is an example of full justification, with the text spaced to align with both the left- and right-hand margins.  Full justification is the default on most word processor packages, looking very neat and professional.

This is an example of right justification which, surprise, surprise, implies that the text is justified to the right-hand margin only.

Finally, this paragraph uses central justification, with the text centrally aligned between the margins. Central justification is most commonly used for titles, headings and lists (such as menus in restaurants).

---

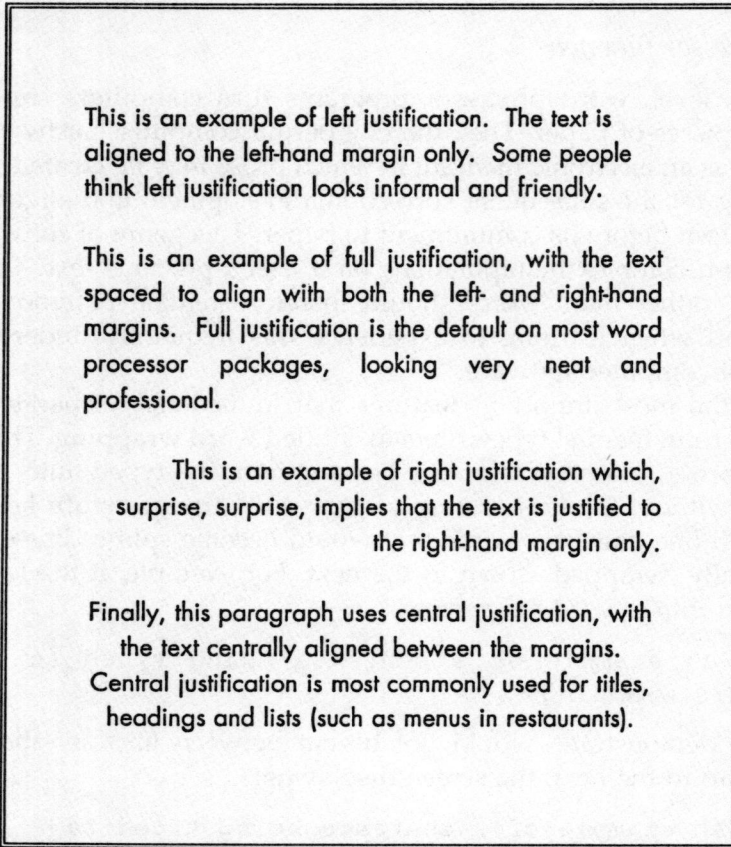

**Figure 2.3**   Word processor justification modes

stage. Page numbering is also carried out automatically, with most programs also offering the ability to print prespecified 'headers' and 'footers' at the top or bottom of every page respectively. This allows, for example, the title of a report to appear on every page of printout. Modern word processors also cope automatically with the placement of footnotes at the base of appropriate pages, and most facilitate the automatic creation of an index via highlighting key words during text preparation.

## Typestyles and fonts

The range of typestyles available in most word processors has increased dramatically in recent years. Even the most basic programs now enable text to appear in *italics*, **bold type**, with <u>underlining</u>, or in a ***<u>combination</u>*** of these styles. Most packages offer many text effects in addition to the above (such as <u>double underlining</u>), although their use is seldom required by most users.

Font control is also highly developed in today's popular word processor packages, with a range of both typefaces and text sizes being available for user selection. Fonts in general are classified under two main headings: **serif** and **sans-serif**. The former categorization includes all typefaces with curved flourishes at their letter ends, a common example being Palatino, as used throughout this *Blueprint*. Sans-serif fonts, on the other hand, have no additions to their letter ends, and often add that extra bit of impact if used sparingly in business documents.

Most word processors specify the size of font selected in points (the larger the point size, the larger the text). The most common type size for the main body of text in a document is between 10 and 12 points: any larger and documents look as if they have been prepared for visually challenged readers, any smaller and recipients may be reaching for their magnifying glasses!

Whilst the variety of fonts and typestyles offered by modern word processors may at first appear a blessing, virgin users should be wary of detracting from the content of their document with too many font or typestyle changes. Most professional documents will use at most two different text fonts (perhaps one for headings and titles and another for the main body of the text). Even design-conscious modern magazines carefully restrict their use of fonts and styles. There is, of course, a message here: don't play with fonts and typestyles unless you have very good reason! A report to the boss using ten different fonts may demonstrate your competence with the office word processor, but it is also likely to convey a rather amateurish impression.

## Text manipulation

In addition to controlling both text and page layout and appearance, word processors offer a range of useful manipulation functions. Simple examples include the ability to search for specified words and phrases, and to permit their automatic replacement with a different term throughout a document. Such facilities must, of necessity, be used with more than a little forethought. Suppose, for example, a novelist had decided to change the name of his main character from William to Harold via automatic replacement. All would be fine until, perhaps, a reference in passing to the Battle of Hastings, wherein the victor would be referred to as Harold the Conqueror!

More complex text manipulation functions include spell checking, an ever-available thesaurus, and even routines to advise on grammatic style. Spell checking functions in particular are a godsend to most users, being just as useful for picking up typing errors as they are in correcting mistakes resulting from lexical ignorance. They must, however, also be relied upon with caution. For example, the term 'downsizing' is unknown to my word processor, the word's replacement with either 'dances' or 'danseuse' constantly being suggested. With lapses of concentration common when spell checking large documents, the replacement of words of which the computer is ignorant with inappropriate 'substitutes' may frequently occur. This problem can be partially overcome if the program in question allows the user to add words to its dictionary file. This facility may in turn create problems, however, if users inadvertently add incorrectly spelt words to their dictionary, thus perpetuating spelling errors in future documents.

Another useful processing function of this software genre is entitled **mailmerge**. This refers to the process whereby a 'personalised' standard letter may be sent to every person on a mailing list, with each recipient receiving correspondence printed with their own name and address. To accomplish this, a list of names and addresses is prepared in one document file, and the standard letter in another, with special codes denoting where the address and customer name should appear. The word processor program then merges these two files together, producing a third document containing one letter for each person included on the mailing list.

## Introducing graphics

Most word processors allow users to import pictorial figures and graphics images from other software packages. Usually, the document's text will automatically flow around imported graphical images, even if they are of an irregular shape. Many word processor programs allow their users to define different types of shading and line style around the perimeter of their graphics images, and some even provide drawing tools for the creation of simple charts and diagrams. The advancing graphics facilities of modern word processors allow users to create very complex, graphically adorned page layouts with relative ease. Where an even greater degree of typographical control and artistic freedom is required, however, the more extensive capabilities of **desktop publishing** (DTP) programs must be called into play.

## Desktop publishers

The divide between word processing and DTP software is, for many, rather blurred. Both program forms, of course, may be used in the process of getting neatly printed words onto paper. A distinction, however, may be plainly cleaved. Word processor programs, on the one hand, are effectively based upon the manipulation of an endless scroll of text that is eventually formatted into pages for output. In contrast, DTP programs are page based, being optimized for text and graphical layout, rather than the input and manipulation of words. DTP program operations thus mirror the actions of traditional page layout artists, with functions such as 'cut' and 'paste' being utilized to rearrange columns of text, headings and graphics images on a page-by-page basis. They also offer a greater range of fonts and typestyles than found in most word processing packages, with more accurate control of line and letter spacing, colour usage, and text and graphics rotation also being available. Common DTP packages for IBM personal computers include:

- *PageMaker*™;
- *Ventura Publisher*™;
- *PagePlus*™; and
- *Quark XPress*™.

Because DTP programs are optimized for page layout rather than text manipulation, large sections of text (such as book chapters) are usually prepared as text data files in a word processor before being imported into a DTP package for final page layout. DTP programs should thus not be viewed as alternatives to word processors (although a powerful word processor such as *WordPerfect 6.0* may reasonably be argued to be an alternative to a DTP package). Therefore, if a user is only to purchase one text-manipulation program, the word processor must come above the DTP option on their software shopping list. A typical screenshot of DTP software in operation is illustrated in figure 2.4, here with *PagePlus 2.0* running under *Windows* being used to create a one-page advertisement.

## DTP and page layout skills

Although in theory DTP programs exist to increase the presentation quality of an organization's printed output, potential users should always bear in mind that the purchase of a DTP package will not instantly endow staff members with creative page layout skills. This is, however, a popular misconception! Whereas nobody in their right mind would purchase a guitar and expect to become an instantly accomplished musician, many people believe that after purchasing a DTP package they will quickly be producing typographical works of art. Like the guitar, of course, any DTP program only provides a means to a creatively driven end. Managers should therefore be wary of switching their publishing workload from specialist artists skilled in page layout techniques to word processor users suddenly provided with a DTP package.

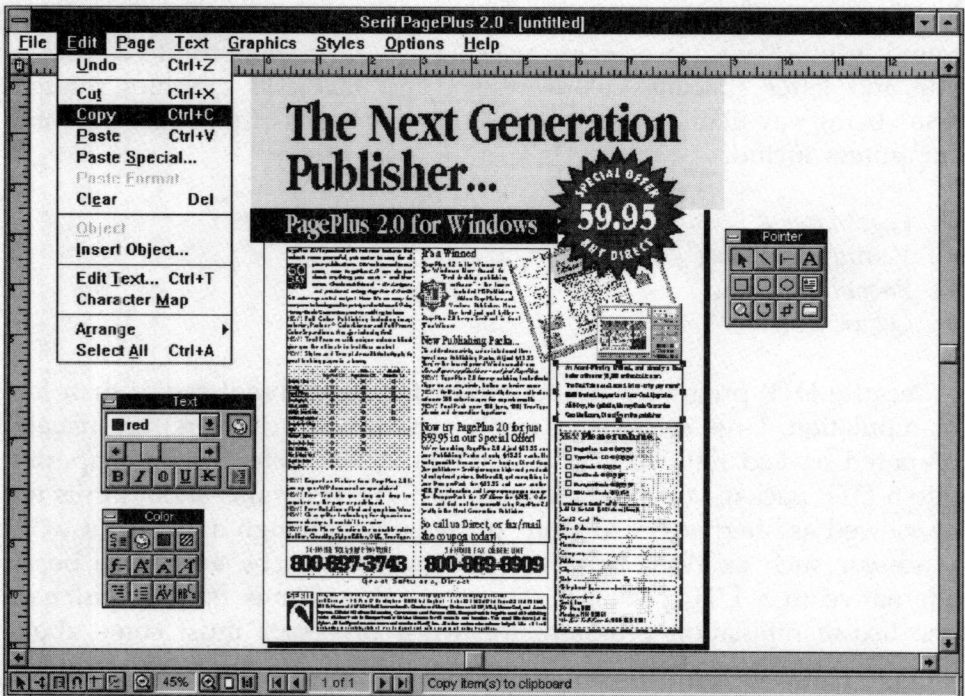

**Figure 2.4**  Desktop publishing with PagePlus 2.0 (Courtesy Serif Inc., 1993)

## Spreadsheet software

After word processing, the most common application of personal computers is for running **spreadsheet** packages. Spreadsheets are effectively the computer software variant of the accountant's old paper ledger, although their application in business is not limited to assignments within the finance department. Indeed, most tasks requiring the presentation and manipulation of numerical data can be entertained with a modern spreadsheet, even though such software is highly intuitive, with its basic operational principle being very easy to master. The most popular spreadsheet packages for the IBM PC at present include:

- *Lotus 1-2-3*™;
- *Quattro Pro*™';
- *Excel*™; and
- *Supercalc*™.

### *The electronic table*

A spreadsheet is basically a computerized table of vertical *columns*, labelled with letters, and horizontal *rows*, referred to by number. At the intersection of columns and rows within this table we find spreadsheet *cells*. Cells may contain either a number, a short item of text (known as a *label*), or some kind of mathematical or logical formula based upon other cell references. Figure 2.5 illustrates a simple spreadsheet with four columns and eight rows. The entry in cell A1 is the text label 'EMPLOYEE', in A3 the label 'Daphne', in B3 the number 20, and so forth. The figures in column D,

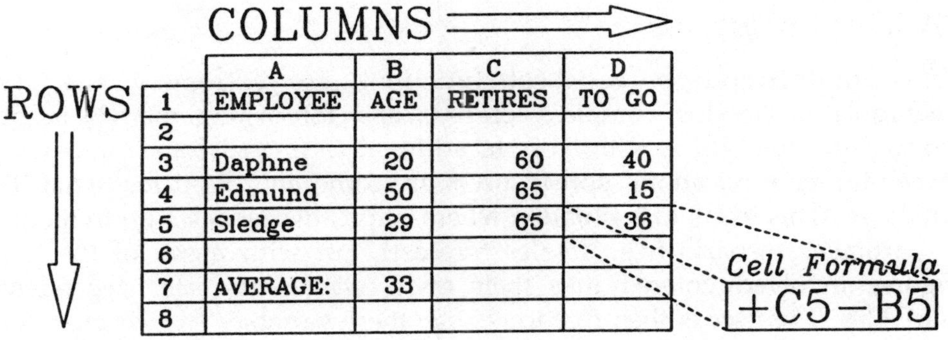

COLUMNS ⟹

| | | A | B | C | D |
|---|---|---|---|---|---|
| ROWS | 1 | EMPLOYEE | AGE | RETIRES | TO GO |
| | 2 | | | | |
| | 3 | Daphne | 20 | 60 | 40 |
| | 4 | Edmund | 50 | 65 | 15 |
| | 5 | Sledge | 29 | 65 | 36 |
| | 6 | | | | |
| | 7 | AVERAGE: | 33 | | |
| | 8 | | | | |

Cell Formula
$+C5-B5$

**Figure 2.5**   Spreadsheet example

however, are derived from spreadsheet formulas. With column B holding a figure for each employee's age, and column C their retirement age, their time 'TO GO' is clearly the latter minus the former. Thus cell D3 will contain the formula +C3-B3, cell D4 the entry +C4-B4, and finally D5 (as illustrated) the formula +C5-B5. Note that there is a '+' sign at the beginning of each formula entry, to indicate to the software that the entry is not to be treated as a text label.

## Formulas and functions

A great many functions may applied to data resident in the spreadsheet software medium. The width of different columns may be altered to accommodate different data forms, sort operations may be instigated to rearrange the data into different formats, and numerous graphs and charts may be directly derived from figures existing in spreadsheet cells.

Totals, averages, data deviations and net present values (as well as a host of other data-dependent figures) may also be automatically produced within spreadsheet software. Most packages accomplish such tasks via so-called @functions. The function @SUM is usually employed to produce totals. For example, @SUM(B3..B5) is the formula for totalling the numerical entries in cells B3, B4 and B5. In a similar vein, @AVG(B3..B5) will calculate the average value across these three cells, and is thus the entry in cell B7 in figure 2.5. What makes spreadsheets particularly powerful is the fact that if one numerical entry is altered by the user, all formulas dependant on its value will also change. Thus, if Daphne's age was altered from 20 to 21 in cell B3 in figure 2.5, the figure in cell D3 would automatically change from 40 to 39.

## 'What-if?' analysis

Once understood, spreadsheet functions are extremely easy to manipulate, allowing complex accounts and forecasting models to be created by most users with ease. In addition to financial and numerical presentation applications, spreadsheets are commonly used for 'what-if? analysis'. This refers to a situation where a spreadsheet is set up to model a particular scenario (e.g. a sales forecast), but with many of the key figures involved entered into their own cells as discrete, dependent variables. The user is then free to change these variables (which may, for example, be raw material costs and interest rate values) with the spreadsheet, to illustrate how their alteration impacts on the rest of the model. A manager can thus pose questions such as 'What if our raw material costs doubled?', and be provided with a new set of figures in a matter of seconds. Spreadsheet programs are therefore common in departments such as strategic planning and market research, as well as in traditionally numerically orientated arenas like accounting and finance. (Hands-on exercises in the operation of the *Lotus 1-2-3* spreadsheet appear in appendix I.)

## Database packages

Whilst word processor and spreadsheet software collect gold and silver medals in the program popularity stakes, **database** applications usually come in third to pick up the bronze. More complex in operation than spreadsheet tables, databases are the most powerful common classification of PC software, and are employed where complex data storage or manipulation is required. Common database packages for IBM PCs include:

- *Paradox*™;
- *dBASE*™; and
- *Dataease*™.

### *Database software advantages*

In essence, database programs simply act as elaborate filing systems. Unlike paper or card files, however, they not only store items of data, but also relationships between stored items. For example, in a paper-based system you may have one file detailing your debtors, and a second file for your address book. Thus, to gain the information required to chase a particular debtor, you would have to consult both files, gaining information on the balance outstanding from one, and address details from the other. Had both files existed in a computer database package, a relational link between the two could have been created, such that when you called up creditor information on screen the relevant address information would also become instantly available.

Database programs with the ability to relate different data files reduce excessive data duplication, as records may be cross-referenced in a great many ways. In contrast, a paper filing card can only sit in one box or filing drawer at any one point in time. The installation of database software on a network of linked PCs also brings the advantage of shared access to central data files. In turn, data security may also be centralized, with access to computer files being easier to control than access to a scattering of paper documents around a large, open-plan office. Finally, computer databases can easily be regularly 'backed-up' (in other words copied to other computers or safe data stores) to insure against fire, theft, food and other disasters. The back-up of a paper-based filing system is a much more daunting task, (and thus seldom undertaken) due to the sheer physical bulk of material involved.

No doubt because they offer so many potential advantages compared to paper-based filing systems, database packages are employed for a wide range of business applications, including:

- personnel filing systems;
- stock control;
- customer records;
- supplier information; and
- accounts ledgers (although dedicated accounts programs are also commonly available).

*Database vocabulary*

Database applications are built around three key design elements: *fields*, *records* and *files*. A database *field* refers to a particular data category within a database, e.g. customer surnames or particular account balances. All the data fields related to one particular person or company then comprise one database *record*, e.g. all the information relating to employee John Smith. Finally, a collection of similarly structured records comprises a database *file*, for example all company supplier records. The concept of database *files* containing *records* which in turn contain *fields* is further illustrated in figures 2.6 and 2.7.

Figure 2.6 shows a small database file containing four employee records, each with four distinct data fields (i.e. Name, Salary, Payroll Ref and Bank Acc/No). Figure 2.7 illustrates a 'card index' analogy of the storage of the same information. Here, the entire database file corresponds to the collection of all the cards in a particular filing drawer (in this case four). Each individual card equates to one single database record, comprised of the appropriate number of fields. John Smith therefore has his own record card with four fields of data entered upon it (as depicted). Most database packages are programmed to display information in this manner, with one record on screen at a time. The screen format for displaying records, as well as the number of field

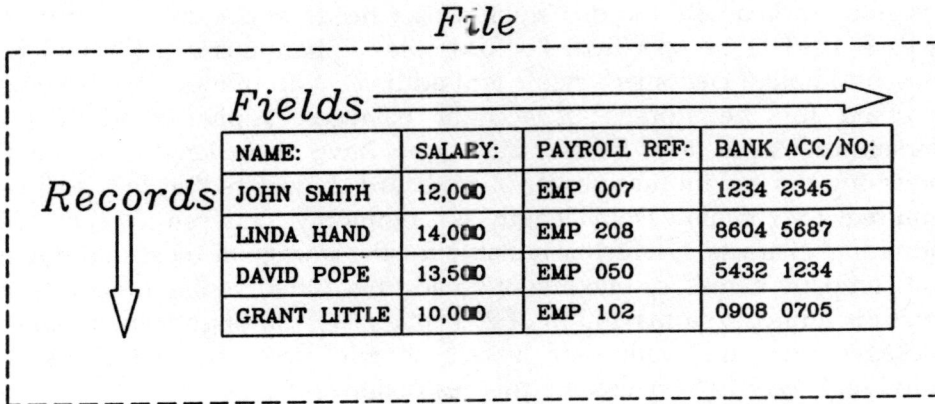

**Figure 2.6** A database table

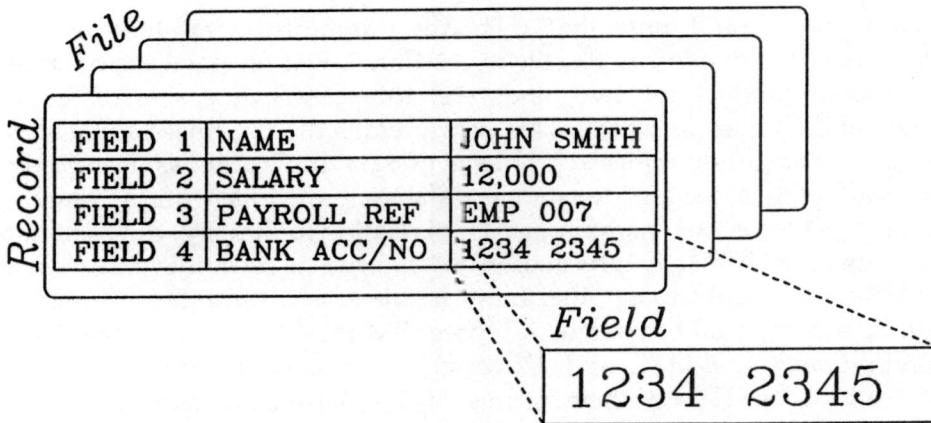

**Figure 2.7** Database 'card index' analogy

types and records in the database file, may usually be customized by the user. This means that there is no common appearance for database programs, unlike spreadsheet packages which always look like on-screen ledger tables.

## Data field types

Database fields may be one of two variants: *numeric* (fields used to hold numbers) or *alphanumeric* (fields used to hold text entries). When designing a database, the first thing a user needs to decide is the nature of each field to be specified. For example, alphanumeric fields will be chosen to hold a customer's name and address, with numeric fields being specified for the storage of account balances. Alphanumeric fields (sometimes called text fields), must also have their length specified, indicating the maximum number of keyboard characters that they will be required to contain. Field length is commonly between 20 and 30 individual characters, which is suitable for the storage of most individual and company names, or one line of an address. Often, alphanumeric field length is limited to a maximum of 255 characters, although some modern packages offer the option of linking longer *'free-form'* text fields to individual records to overcome this restriction.

## *Flat-file versus relational systems*

Finally, we should note that database programs themselves may be encountered in two forms: flat-file or **relational**. Flat-file database packages are the simplest of the two, and refer to systems incapable of linking different data files (or tables). This clearly limits their business application, as such packages do not ease problems of data duplication as discussed at the start of this section. Relational databases are much more common, being capable (as their name suggests) of relating (or linking) different data files together. Thus, if information is changed in one file (such as an address book), links to all other files capable of accessing this information will be automatically updated. All three IBM PC database packages listed herein (*Paradox, dBASE* and *Dataease*) are relational, and readers are advised to steer clear of their far less flexible flat-file ancestors.

## Design and graphics packages

The graphics capabilities of personal computers have expanded rapidly in the past few years, leading to the development of a broad spectrum of software applications geared towards image production. Ignoring games programs that fly space-invaders across your VDU or simulate the last battle for civilization as we know it, such packages fall into three distinct categories:

- presentation graphics packages;
- **computer-aided design** (CAD) and structured drawing packages; and
- bitmap graphics packages.

## Presentation graphics packages

Presentation graphics packages are probably the ones most likely to be encountered by the business user. They are capable of producing a range of charts and graphs, from imported data if required, in a rapid and professional fashion. A variety of standard chart and graph formats are always available, aiding the creation of pie-charts, bar graphs, bullet-lists and other common output forms. Simple drawing tools are also provided, enabling the construction of figures from lines, circles, boxes and other basic shapes. These drawing tools also permit graphs derived from user data to be augmented with additional titles, arrows and labels.

The application of presentation graphics packages ranges from the production of overhead and even 35 mm slides, to the creation of diagrams for import into word processor or DTP documents. Because they are intended to be easy to use in a variety of ways, presentation graphics packages are not suitable for complex design or illustration work. Common examples of such software for the IBM PC include:

- *Harvard Graphics*™; and
- *Freelance*™.

## CAD and structured graphics packages

CAD packages allow computers to be applied to complex drafting and modelling applications. They are thus suitable for architectural and engineering drawing, and for the design of anything from machine components to yoghurt pots or country cottages.

CAD programs that can only work in two dimensions (i.e. that can only produce flat drawings) are sometimes referred to as *structured drawing packages*. They usually include functions such as automatic dimensioning, and allow complex plans to be built up on many different drawing levels. Font and text control are rarely as advanced in CAD packages as in presentation graphics software. If you need to produce line illustrations, however, then a 2-D CAD package is usually the best software choice. Three common 2-D PC CAD packages are:

- *Autosketch*™ (used to produce many of the figures in this book);
- *TurboCAD*™; and
- *AutoCAD*™.

Three-dimensional CAD packages produce on-screen solid models that can be rotated and viewed from many angles. They allow, for example, an architect to 'walk through' a building before it is actually constructed. Complex 3-D graphics and design modelling applications still require very powerful computer hardware if they are to run effectively, often being dependent on mini, mainframe or even supercomputers rather than humble PCs. With the ever-increasing power of desktop computers, however, it is likely that in the not-too-distant future complex 3-D CAD packages will be running quite happily on office machines.

### Bitmap graphics packages

Both presentation graphics and CAD packages produce what are commonly termed *structured* or *vector-based* images. This means that their drawings are stored in a precise mathematical form of coordinates and lines. Once constructed, each drawing element can be manipulated and resized any number of times without losing any of its detail. Such an approach is critical for line drawings and graphs liable to be exported between different software packages, with their size being tailored to fit the final layout in question.

An alternative means of computer image creation involves the manipulation of the individual coloured squares, or **pixels**, from which computer and video displays are formed. A typical computer screen image, for example, is composed of a pixel grid 640 squares horizontally by 400 vertically. When stored as pixel grids, computer images are referred to as *bitmaps* – a mapping of the individual bits of information comprising the picture. If increased in size, a bitmapped object will always decrease in detail, as the small squares of which it is composed become larger. After enlargement, images will thus appear with jagged rather than smooth edges.

Bitmap graphics are generally used when images will never be seen other than on computer or television screens, or where complex colour or shading effects are required. Common applications include **desktop video** (DTV) work, the creation of high-quality slides with gradient-shaded backgrounds, or the manipulation of photo-realistic images for DTP. PC bitmap graphics packages include:

- *Deluxe Paint*$^{TM}$;
- *CorelDRAW*$^{TM}$; and
- *Autodesk Animator*$^{TM}$ (used to create moving images).

## Other common packages

Most of the time, 95 per cent of PC users use their machines to run the type of word processing, DTP, spreadsheet, database and graphics applications so far outlined. Other business software genres do exist, however, with publishers always seeking new 'killer applications' with which to improve their market share.

### Accounts software

Although many PC users, especially in small companies, operate accounts systems using standard spreadsheets or databases, dedicated accounts software is available. These packages are basically preprogrammed database systems, with entry screens, ledger tables and the relational links between them predefined. By far the most common suite of PC accounts packages come under the umbrella title of *Sage*™.

### Integrated packages

More of a variant than a genre, integrated software packages combine the functions of other major software types. Most integrated packages include a word processor, spreadsheet, database, and some graphics facilities. The advantage of such software is the ease with which data can be moved between different program modules (e.g. the export of a spreadsheet table into a word processor document). The disadvantage is that the individual program modules are not as sophisticated as full-blown dedicated programs. Common on home PCs, integrated packages offer excellent value for money, and are bundled free with machines by some PC suppliers. *Microsoft*® *Works*™ is probably the most common example of such software for IBM computers.

### Project and time management packages

Programs that allow users to keep track of appointments, or even the progress of long-term projects, are becoming increasingly popular with a generation weaned on personal organizers and databank watches. Others adamantly resist the introduction of this type of software, alarmed that the computer will tell them what to do, and will allow others access to their appointment schedule. Project management software can look very impressive on screen, with colourful linked bar charts indicating the progression of dependent tasks. Of most use to those involved with construction, research and other large-scale one-off work activities, project and time management packages are unlikely to become widespread. A common example of their ilk for the IBM PC is *SuperProject*™.

## Communications packages

With the increasing interconnection of personal computers, programs that facilitate the easy transfer of information between users are becoming a popular, if not essential, component of office systems. In particular, **electronic mail** (e-mail) software for sending messages between networked users is now widespread. With computer network and communication technologies such an important growth area, the hardware and software concerned are explored separately in chapter 4.

## Summary

This chapter has:

- Differentiated between applications software and low-level programs, such as operating systems.
- Outlined the nature of MS-DOS and the *Windows* WIMP environment
- Detailed the nature of the following key genres of business software:
    - word processors and desktop publishers;
    - spreadsheets;
    - databases;
    - graphics packages; and
    - accounts, integrated and time/project management software.

## Review questions

1.  Explain the difference between: (a) word processors and desktop publishers; and (b) spreadsheet and database packages.
2.  For a data storage application of which you are aware (e.g. personnel record filing), specify the nature (and, if appropriate, character length) of each required data field.

# 3 Personal computer hardware

Although there is a fair degree of diversity in the range of software employed by business computer users, the hardware on which most applications are run is remarkably uniform. This chapter explores common personal computer hardware, detailing the specification of IBM PC and compatible machines, as well as the array of peripheral hardware available for additional connection. A broad attempt is made to help anybody engaged in the purchase of personal computer hardware for business or home use, and by the end of this chapter the reader should at least be able to comprehend machine specifications printed in supplier catalogues and magazine advertisements. Finally, the more popular non-IBM personal computer platforms found occupying distinct niche segments in the personal computer market come in for some scrutiny.

## A typical configuration

Before delving into specifics, it is perhaps best to consider the configuration of a typical personal computer system as found in residence on many an office desk. Figure 3.1 illustrates such a desktop hardware conglomeration, based around an IBM PC (or compatible) computer with a VDU monitor and a typewriter-style keyboard. The machine possesses an internal hard disk to store applications programs and data, and a floppy disk drive to allow storage on removable media. Additionally, the PC is equipped with a mouse to ease the operation of a WIMP environment such as *Microsoft*® *Windows*™, and a printer for the production of hardcopy. This collection of hardware is really the bare minimum with which to do anything productive in the 1990s, with more and more items of peripheral hardware likely to be found adorning the average PC as we move towards the next century.

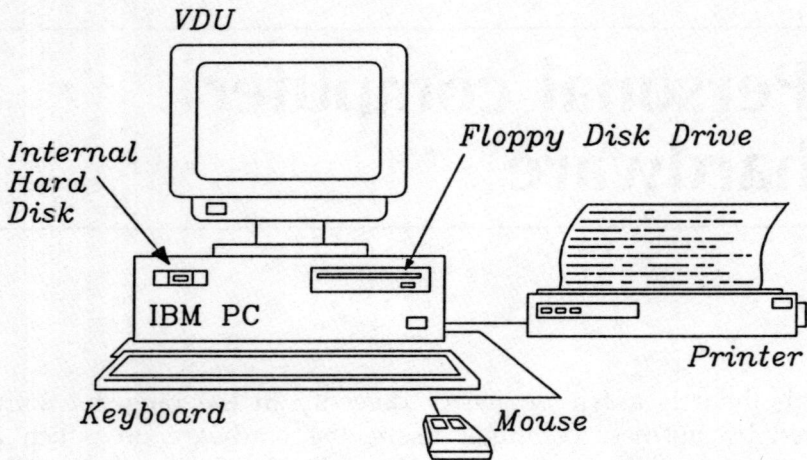

**Figure 3.1** Typical desktop hardware

## The IBM PC

Launched in 1981, the IBM PC quickly came to dominate business computing. After-sales service was excellent, the software available of high quality, and a reputation for reliability was soon spawned. IBM also allowed the architecture of their PC to be open, paving the way for other manufacturers to copy the design of its innards and produce compatible computers. Such PCs, built in a modular form from basic components by a myriad of firms worldwide, are commonly termed IBM 'compatibles', or 'clones'. To ease linguistics herein, the term 'IBM PC' will be used to refer to any machine either produced by IBM, or with a compatible hardware architecture. Even though most PCs are no longer produced by International Business Machines, their initials remain synonymous with the hardware platform spawned by 'Big Blue' over a decade ago.

### The central processing unit

Two critical factors made it easy for other manufacturers to produce IBM PC-compatible systems. The first was that the IBM PC's operating system had been developed for/with IBM by Microsoft Corporation, who made versions available to other PC suppliers. On the hardware side, IBM PCs were based upon a range of microprocessors and associated microchips produced by electronics giant Intel. All modern PCs rely on one microprocessor, or **central processing unit** (CPU), to coordinate their activities and undertake data operations. With the component 'heart' of the IBM PC on the open market, the production of compatible machines was greatly eased. Over the past decade Intel's range of CPU chips have themselves been cloned, further facilitating the spread of IBM compatible computers.

As time has progressed, the CPU chips on which IBM PCs have been based have become ever-more powerful, in turn bestowing their host computers with increased capabilities. The microprocessor chip on which a PC is based is central to its overall specification. Early IBM PCs, named XTs, were based upon the 8088 microprocessor, with later machines using the faster 8086 processor chip. Then IBM developed its so-called AT computers, based upon Intel's more advanced 80286 CPU, and operating about four times faster than the first XT machines. Soon on the heels of these computers came yet more powerful PCs with 80386 chips at their heart, and then in the 1990s PCs based around 80486 chips. Thus, when people talk about **286**, **386** or **486** PCs they are simply referring to machines based around 80286, 80386 or 80486 microprocessors respectively. Finally (at present), we have the emergence of the **Pentium** chip as the successor to the 80486. Interestingly, this CPU was to have been named the 80586, until Intel discovered that numbers were more difficult to uphold as trademarks. The change of name from '80586' to 'Pentium' was therefore undertaken in an attempt to prevent other manufacturers producing clone 586 CPUs. Figure 3.2 depicts the progression of Intel CPU chips used at the heart of the IBM PC.

## SX and DX chips

To confuse computer purchasers still further, in the late 1980s the 80386 chip became available in a cut-down version known as the 80386-SX, with its more powerful cousin being renamed the 80386-DX. Within advertisements and supplier catalogues, computer buyers will come across 386-SX and 386-DX machines, and similarly 486-SX and 486-DX PCs. All that need be remembered is that SX chips run slower than DX chips – thus readers should seek out DX chip PCs if at all possible. That said, a 486-SX PC will usually run faster than a 386-DX machine.

## Processor speed

When comparing PC specifications, the speed at which the CPU runs (or is *clocked*) must also be taken into account. Processor speed is measured in

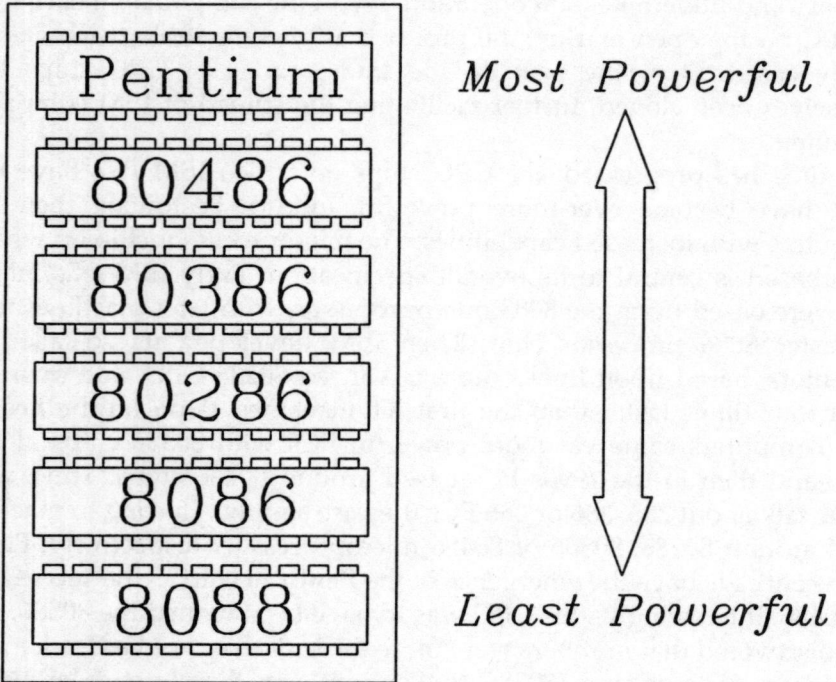

**Figure 3.2**  Intel CPU progression

megahertz (MHz): the faster the speed quoted, the quicker software applications run. The speed indicates the number of CPU operations being carried out per second. Thus a 16 MHz 386-SX PC runs slower than a 25 MHz 386-SX machine. Problems arise, however, with speed comparisons between PCs with different hardware configurations. Especially acute are problems in comparing the operational speed of 80386- and 80486-based PCs. A **landmark speed** is sometimes provided in addition to clock speed by PC suppliers, derived from a program that attempts to gauge how fast applications packages will actually run. A typical 486-SX PC running at 20 MHz may perhaps be quoted as having a landmark speed of 67 MHz, for comparison with a 20 MHz 386-SX machine (landmark speed around 25 MHz), or a 33 MHz 386-DX PC (landmarked at 47 MHz). Claims and counter-claims abound as to the integrity of landmark speed indicators, and depend to some extent on the type of software applications for which a PC will be utilized. Users concerned with such speed factors are probably best to curtail any arguments and simply purchase the fastest 486-DX PC they can find, or even a Pentium-based machine if available.

## Maths co-processor chips

It should also be noted that for number-crunching processing operations a PC's speed may be greatly enhanced via the introduction of a chip known as a **maths co-processor**. This is effectively a microchip working in tandem with the main CPU to do all its hard sums! Thus, when the CPU at a PC's heart is required to perform a complex mathematical calculation, it trades it out to the co-processor chip and gets on with other processing operations until an answer is returned. Adding a maths co-processor to a computer effectively allows outsourcing to occur at the micro silicon level! Users who regularly crunch lots of figures are advised to purchase computers with maths co-processors fitted. It should be noted that not all applications programs are written to take advantage of co-processor chips, and even those that are may require users to run special set-up routines. Software manuals therefore need consulting (a sacrilegious act for many users!) when a weary CPU is to be aided by a maths co-processor.

## Modern specifications

A 386-SX PC running clocked at least 16 MHz is probably the minimum specification hardware a buyer should now consider, even though numerous business users are still contentedly using 80286–based computers. Many computer suppliers, on the other hand, deem even the 80386 chip 'dead', and will only supply PCs based around 486-SX CPUs and upwards. Ultimately, buyers pays their money and takes their choice. Providing the machine comfortably runs the software for which it was purchased (and *very* few business applications *need* a CPU more powerful than a 386 to drive them adequately), then that is all that matters. What purchasers must be wary of is moon-chasing – paying way over budget for higher-spec PCs that 'will never become obsolete, Sir'. They will, of course – and quickly. Where computer hardware is concerned, short-term obsolescence in terms of speed and power is an absolute dead certainty.

## Memory

Processor type and speed are not the only factors to bear in mind when comparing IBM PC specifications. The amount of memory available is also critical, influencing not only whether a particular program will run, but also its speed of operation. As a general rule, the more memory a PC has available the better.

**Table 3.1** IBM PC display formats

| Format | Characteristics | Comments |
|--------|-----------------|----------|
| **MDA** (Monochrome Display Adaptor) | Monochrome text only – no graphics capabilities | Now obsolete |
| **CGA** (Colour Graphics Adaptor) | Displays both text and graphics in up to 16 colours. Highest graphics resolution 320 × 200 pixels. | Only found on very old desktop PCs, and some cheap portables. |
| **Hercules** | High-resolution, high-quality, monochrome display for both text and graphics. Graphics resolution 720 × 348 pixels. | Good display if you don't want colour images, although rapidly disappearing. |
| **EGA** (Enhanced Graphics Adaptor) | Displays both text and graphics in up to 16 colours. Highest graphics resolution 640 × 400 pixels. | Until a few years back the industry standard. Perfectly adequate for most DOS-based business applications. |
| **VGA** (Video Graphics Array) | High-resolution text and graphics display with up to 256 colours on screen simultaneously. Highest graphics resolution 640 × 480 pixels. | Now accepted as the default standard for IBM PC displays. Minimum requirement for successful *Windows* operation. |
| **SVGA** (Super Video Graphics Array) | Improvement on the VGA standard, displaying high-resolution text and graphics in up to 256 colours from a palette of 16.7 million. Highest graphics resolution 800 × 600 pixels. | Widely accepted standard offering a higher resolution than VGA. Full capabilities rarely used by most DOS programs. Excellent for *Windows*. If you have the choice, opt for SVGA. |

The smallest meaningful unit of computer memory is the **byte**, equivalent to one character of computer storage. Until a few years back, a PC's memory was expressed in **kilobytes**, with 1Kb being equivalent to $2^{10}$ (1024) bytes. 1Kb of memory thus stores just over 1000 characters, equivalent to around 120 words of a word processed document. Early IBMb XT PCs had either 512 or 640Kb of **RAM** (random access memory) used to store their programs and data. Nowadays, with greater memory capacities widespread, PC memory is usually expressed in **megabytes**, with 1Mb equivalent to 1024Kb. 386-based PCs and above are commonly fitted with either 2, 4 or 8Mb of RAM – with 2Mb being the minimum required to run applications properly under *Microsoft*® *Windows*™. It should be noted that the contents of a computer's RAM are lost when the machine's power is switched off. RAM is thus not a form of permanent data storage.

## *Graphics and display formats*

In parallel with developments in CPU power and RAM capacity over the past decade, the ability of the IBM PC to display high-resolution colour graphics has also increased. The graphics resolution of a PC refers to the size of the pixel grid used to create images on-screen. Resolution is expressed by the number of screen co-ordinates vertically by the number horizontally. Early PCs created images on a grid typically 320 × 200 pixels in resolution, and could only display monochrome images (usually green on black or amber on black). Modern machines use a much higher resolution pixel grid to display their images – typically 640 × 480 or even 800 × 600 pixels in size. Hundreds of colours may be displayed on screen simultaneously, selected from a palette (colour range) of over 16 million different hues.

The display capabilities of any PC depend on the format of graphics card fitted. Graphics cards fit internally inside the main PC housing, and may be removed and replaced with a higher-specification board if required. Such modularity is a key characteristic of IBM PC construction, enabling major components to be removed, replaced and upgraded with ease.

Six graphics formats – MDA, CGA, Hercules, EGA, VGA, SVGA – are most common, with cards of these standards being found inside the majority of IBM PCs in existence. Table 3.1 details the progression and characteristics of each graphics standard, with VGA (the Video Graphics Array) being the minimum format a user should settle for when purchasing a new computer.

## Peripheral hardware

The main areas of IBM PC hardware specification of which all users should be aware (CPU type, CPU speed, RAM capacity and graphics format) have now been detailed. Attention can therefore be switched to the range of additional, **peripheral hardware** that may be connected to personal computers. With reference to our earlier model of the computer as a data system (chapter 1, figure 1.1), peripheral hardware may be subdivided into three distinct categories:

- input hardware;
- output hardware; and
- storage devices.

Each of the above peripheral device categorizations will now be explored in turn, although it should be noted that some items of hardware fall between clean subdivisions. (A touch-sensitive monitor screen, for example, may be used for both input and output purposes.) Readers should also be aware that peripheral devices used for computer networking and communications are excluded from the following and detailed separately in chapter 4.

## Input hardware

### The keyboard

By far the most common, if not the most obvious, means of getting information into a computer is via a keyboard. The basic design has gone unchanged for decades, with characters arranged in the QWERTY layout first devised for manual typewriters. In addition to the keys provided on their typewriter ancestors, computer keyboards feature a line of *function keys* (used to operate program functions!) most commonly along the top of the main keyblock. On full-size keyboards there is also a *numeric keypad* on the far right to facilitate faster numerical entry for users familiar with a calculator pad. Extra keys, such as control (Ctrl) and alternate (Alt) are also provided to enable additional key combinations to be obtained.

Many books feature some tale or legend explaining why early typewriter keyboards were arranged in the QWERTY fashion. This one does not, as no two of these myths appear consistent! What is agreed across literatures is that the QWERTY layout is not ideal for very rapid typing in terms of both operator comfort and entry speed. Thus, every six months or so, a new keyboard design appears in the computer press featuring new contours, key formations, wrist supports or even hinges! A famous example is the 'Malatron' keyboard, shaped around two human hands. Such new, 'improved' keyboards have yet to catch on, with the cost of hardware replacement and operator retraining far outweighing any ergonomic advantages. As long as the keyboard is with us, therefore, it is a safe bet that its QWERTY layout will remain unaltered.

## The mouse

Ten years ago, few office workers would have predicted their modern contemporaries being perfectly content with mice resident upon their office desks. The variant of mouse now common is, of course, plastic and inanimate, being used to move a **cursor** or **pointer** around a computer screen. Handy buttons atop the device enable menus and other options to be selected. The only similarity between the computer mouse and the apparently cheese-fixated rodent of cartoon fame is the resemblance of the cable of the former to the tail of the latter. Even then, the impersonation is somewhat dubious – though the purchase of furry covers can help a great deal.

Metaphors aside, the mouse is an increasingly important item of input hardware. WIMP environments in particular are very difficult to operate successfully without a mouse connected to the PC. Similarly, most DTP and graphics packages are easier to operate with a plastic desk companion in hand, and even word processor and spreadsheet operation can be improved. Like them or loathe them, mice have invaded late twentieth-century desks to stay.

Computer mice operate by either one of two principles. Most simply feature a rubber-coated ball in their base rotated by movement over a contact surface. Rollers then convey input information back to the computer. Mice that work in this manner must have their ball cleaned regularly, or else dust and dirt will clog it up and prevent smooth on-screen movements. A foam or rubber *mouse mat* (even if adorned with a naff supplier logo) may also be utilized improve operation.

Other species of mice have no moving parts, and instead trace operator actions via firing infrared beams back and forth at a special mouse mat etched with fine reflective lines. This system is more accurate than the rolling-ball based system, though damage to (or loss of) the special mouse mat renders it inoperable.

## *Trackballs and other mouse alternatives*

Like a mouse, a trackball is used to move the pointer or cursor around a computer screen. They are effectively upside-down mice, with movement being achieved via manipulation of a large top-mounted sphere while the trackball itself remains stationary. Trackballs can be more difficult to control than mice, and are inadvisable for use in on-screen drawing.

The main advantage of a trackball over its rodent cousin is that it requires far less desk space in which to operate, and may even be manipulated in mid-air. A trackball can also be built into the main computer keyboard, meaning the device is always at hand. Such trackballs are common on portable computers, where a trailing mouse and mat would be inconvenient. Also growing in popularity are tiny 'thumb-balls' that may be attached to the side of existing keyboards. Finally wand-like *pen-mice* input devices may also be encountered. These again feature a rotating ball, and are 'stroked' across the desk surface in order to move the pointer on screen.

## *The joystick*

Mentioned here only for the sake of comprehensive hardware coverage, a joystick may be attached to a PC for the control of arcade software and simulations programs. If sighted in the workplace, a joystick is unlikely to find business application other than in games playing to relieve office tension!

## *Graphics tablets and pen-based systems*

For accurate on-screen drawing work neither a mouse nor a trackball will suffice. For applications such as CAD a pressure-sensitive **graphics tablet** may well to be used for drawing input. These devices are usually A4, A3 or sometimes A2 in size, and drawn on with a special stylus by the operator. Stylus or pen-based hardware is predicted as the input medium of the future, with a few handheld computers now featuring displays that also function as stylus input grids. In future users will simply be able to write on their computer screens to effect input, scribbling away just as they would with pen and paper.

## Scanners

**Scanners** are hardware devices used to capture graphical data from existing printed or hand-drawn material. They come in two forms. The first is the *hand scanner*, a small device moved by hand over a picture or page of text to enable its capture into a PC. The price of hand scanners has fallen dramatically in recent years, with non-colour devices now retailing at under £100. Scan width is usually limited to 4", however, and accuracy depends on how smoothly the device is moved over the image to be captured. This said, image-processing software is usually supplied to enable large images to be scanned in strips and pasted together.

More expensive computer scanners are of the *flatbed* genre, and operate rather like small photocopiers (the scan-capture process being very similar). An image to be scanned is thus placed on a glass plate, with most flatbed scanners accommodating paper either A4 or A3 in size. Very expensive flatbed scanners, as used for DTP work, will scan images in full colour, and sometimes also operate as photocopiers and colour printers.

Increasingly used in conjunction with both types of scanner is *optical character recognition* (OCR) software. This allows scanned text to be turned into a file suitable for retrieval into a word processor, thus saving the laborious rekeying of printed matter. The other major use for scanners, of course, is in the capture of images for import into word processor documents or DTP layouts.

## Digitizer hardware

Digitizer hardware can also be used to input real-world data into a computer system, and may be either video or audio in format. *Video digitizers*, not surprisingly, capture computer graphics images from a camera or video recorder output. They therefore allow moving and 3-D images to be imported into a computer. Common applications include DTV (desktop video) work and the capture of employee 'photographs' for personnel databases. Special cameras are now also available which capture images electronically, rather than on film, for direct transfer into a computer system.

Finally, *audio digitizers* allow sound information to be entered into a computer. Musicians now commonly use audio digitizer hardware to record music directly to computer memory. The speech recognition systems of natural language computers will also rely on audio digitizers to capture incoming sounds for processing, although such systems are still very much in their infancy.

### MICR, magnetic strip and barcode readers

For the quick, convenient and largely automatic capture of computer input, a variety of devices have been developed which many unknowing computer users have come to take for granted. **MICRs** (magnetic ink character readers) are predominantly used in banks to aid cheque sorting, and read the special digit notation printed in mildly magnetic ink on all cheques. Cheque sorting by such devices is very rapid – processing rates of 2500 per minute are possible.

*Magnetic strip readers* commonly gather information off credit-card magnetic strips. They are of course used in all cashpoint machines, as well as being common for reading employee ID cards in both automatic door locks and other security systems. Finally, *barcode readers* gather input from the thick-and-thin stripe codings printed on everything these days from tins of beans to magazines and production-line components. Most automated stock control systems identify items with barcodes read by suitable readers. Supermarket tills are also clearly dependent upon such hardware, and barcode readers have been noted in design offices wherein all folios and drawings may be bar-coded for easy identification.

## Output hardware

### The CRT monitor

Just as the keyboard is the obvious computer input device, so the **CRT** (cathode ray tube) monitor is the most obvious hardware unit for presenting computer output. Monitors come in a range of sizes, resolutions and price brackets. For PC usage, a monitor must be capable of displaying the output type derived from the PC's graphics card. If a computer is fitted with a VGA display adaptor, for example, then a VGA monitor must be connected to the machine. Monitors thus come in the same range of formats as the graphics cards listed in table 3.1. Common screen sizes are 14' diagonally (the same size as most portable televisions), with 20' or above screens being used in high-quality DTP or CAD systems.

Questions are continually being raised regarding the safety of long-term, close-up exposure to CRT VDU screens. CRT screens, utilizing high-voltage coils to fire electrons at their phosphor display, are known to emit various wavebands of radiation, although studies to determine the degree of hazard are at present inconclusive. Radiation concerns have been one factor driving research into different formats of computer display, as has the need to develop more compact, lower-power display types for portable computers.

## *Liquid crystal displays*

The most common formats of non-CRT screen are based upon liquid crystal technology, enabling flat screens to be produced traditionally displaying dark grey characters on a lighter grey background. Most portable computers use such **LCD**s (liquid crystal displays), with each screen element being a tiny, current-activated crystal in a larger display matrix.

The clarity and speed of LCD screens has long been a problem, with text tending to 'smudge' when scrolled up the display, the viewing angle being small, and the cursor in particular being difficult to locate. Recently *twisted crystal displays* have been developed, offering improved clarity from adapted technology. *Retardation film displays* are also an improvement on basic LCD screens, with greatly improved display contrast. Backlighting is further employed on some LCD-based portable computers to improve the display quality, although this rapidly drains battery life and thus reduces potential portable usage.

Most LCD screens are monochrome only, typically offering sixteen shades of grey in which to render their output. Colour LCD displays also exist, although there are still contrast problems and the screens are expensive to produce in large sizes. Many analysts believe, however, that improvements in LCD technology will continue until most displays will be of this format.

## *Gas plasma displays*

Gas plasma display screens are a much more expensive type of flat screen technology. They display in monochrome only, with bright amber characters on a dark brown background. Common on some up-market portable computers (notably the Toshiba range), the only disadvantage of the gas plasma display is that it requires mains power to operate. Machines with this display format will thus never be truly portable, although their screens are far more comfortable to read than those based upon LCD technology.

## Overhead projection panels

When charged with giving a presentation, an *overhead projection panel* may be placed upon a normal overhead projector to display computer output to a wider audience. These display panels are simply transparent LCD screens, through which light from the OHP's bulb passes for projection. Available in both monochrome and colour graphics formats, overhead projection panels can be very effective presentation aids.

## Video output

The monitor signal produced by most personal computers cannot be directly connected to a normal television, video recorder or video projection system. For some purposes, however, composite or even broadcast-quality video signals will be required, especially where DTV applications are concerned. The price of IBM PC video adaptors is now falling as demand for video output increases. Also becoming common are **genlocks** – items of hardware for combining computer graphics with 'real' video for the creation of title sequences and special-effects presentations.

## Hardcopy hardware

Thus far, all output devices mentioned have been concerned with the immediate, on-screen display of computer data. The other major category of computer output hardware encompasses all devices capable of making marks on paper or film – in other words, printers.

Over the years, office printers have relied upon a variety of technologies, with two general categories of printer commonly being subdivided:

- impact printers; and
- non-impact printers.

## Dot matrix printers

**Dot matrix printers** (DMPs) are the most common form of impact printer. Marks are made on paper by a row of pins thumping an ink-impregnated fabric ribbon against the paper. This row of pins is situated in a *print head* that moves back and forth across the paper, line by line, in order to build up letters from many small dots. The quality of output from a dot matrix printer depends on the size and number of pins in the print head: the smaller the pins and the greater their number, the neater the final output will appear. Two print-head sizes have reigned almost universal over the last decade, 9 pin and 24 pin, the latter being more expensive but offering higher print quality.

The advantage of dot matrix printers is that they are cheap, reliable and can print multi-copy simultaneously via the use of multi-part forms (a crucial advantage when producing invoices). The disadvantages, on the other hand, are that dot matrix printers are noisy and paper jams not uncommon.

## *Daisywheel printers*

The second, and by now extinction-threatened, type of impact printer is the **daisywheel**. Here the print head contains a wheel of letters, which is rotated during printing so that the required character may be impacted against the ribbon and paper. Because letters are not built up from a pattern of dots, the quality of daisywheel printing is very high. These printers are relatively slow, however, and majorly disadvantaged because they can not produce graphical output. In a world increasingly keen to have pictures scattered around document text, the daisywheel printer is thus a dying breed.

## *Ink-jet printers*

Ink-jet printing technology (also in a form known as *bubble-jet*) as been the output hardware triumph of the early 1990s. Ink-jets, coming under our non-impact printer heading, spray ink onto paper, achieving very high quality results together with near-silent operation. In the home and low-end office market, this printer genre has largely taken over from dot matrix technology, with high-quality output now being affordable to the majority. Even superb colour ink-jet printers are not in an out-of-this-world, mortgage-required price bracket.

Ink-jet printers can be overpraised, although few owners ever say a word against them. Firstly, an ink-jet printer is far more expensive to run than a dot matrix machine (costing several pence per page of output, rather than a mere fraction of a penny). Their non-impact technology also prevents the production of multi-copy output. Thirdly, the ink used is usually water-soluble, making it dangerous to print address labels on an ink-jet printer. Finally, ink-jet printers, again due to the ink type, will not print on most photocopier polyester films.

## Laser printers

The high-end non-impact printer variant is the **laser** – the only choice of hardcopy device for high-capacity office usage. Laser printers work via a Xerox process, with a laser beam etching an image on a drum which then picks up minute toner particles to be heat-transferred to a sheet of paper. Printing speed from laser hardware is high, quality excellent, and the graphics capabilities are frequently superb.

Because a whole page is formed and printed in one go from a drum around which paper sheets are rolled, lasers are sometimes known as *page printers*, especially within the DTP community. Also due to the fact that an entire page is constructed before output commences, lasers require a reasonable amount of internal RAM if large graphics images are to be printed. Many 'cheap' laser printers are supplied with 512Kb of memory, although 1Mb of RAM is preferable if extensive graphics printing is to be attempted.

## Other hardcopy devices

Two specialist hardcopy-producing devices are also worthy of note. The first is the *plotter*, which moves a pen over an area of paper to produce slow but high-quality drawing output. Most plotters feature a range of pens, offering multi-colour drawing. They are also most interesting to watch in operation! Mainly used in CAD applications, plotters are essential where large or finely detailed plans are the order of the day.

For presentation purposes, *35 mm slide makers* may be connected to a PC, to render computer graphics direct to 35 mm film stock. Although, in theory, this technology will become obsolete as more and more people switch to using video projectors or overhead projection panels, 35 mm slides are an established presentation media. Few companies need to purchase in-house slide-producing output hardware, as many bureau exist who will accept graphics on disk to be turned into 35 mm slides.

## Additional output forms

In addition to visual and paper formats of computer output, two other increasingly widespread modes are commonly utilized The first is audio output, covering applications as diverse as the production of computer-generated music to complex speech synthesis. Standards for audio output hardware are sadly still in their infancy as far as the IBM PC are concerned, with early designers failing to give the PC audio abilities above a simple 'beep' alarm. Interestingly, it has been the recent acceptance of the IBM PC as a leisure as well as business machine that has prompted the development of sound-output cards (such as the Sound Blaster). Games players, being a particularly demanding user breed, get distinctly unhappy if their aliens do not explode in high-quality stereo! Business applications for audio output hardware are now bound to increase, with desktop PCs being more and more likely to talk in addition to providing visual or hardcopy output.

The final common form of computer output is so obvious it is often forgotten, and includes all areas of computer motion and device control. Most modern factories, for example, have robots under computer manipulation. 'Intelligent buildings', with all electrical devices from air-conditioners to coffee-makers under computer jurisdiction are also being constructed in Japan.

## Storage devices

Capturing, processing and outputting computer data is all very well, but an important element of computer application concerns the reliable storage of programs and information when the computer itself is switched off. Without the availability of storage devices, the usefulness of any computer system is heavily diminished.

### Disk drive storage

The task of retaining computer data is most commonly delegated to some form of disk drive technology. Many disk media formats and hardware devices are now available, although the most common still remain removable floppy disks and the faster, higher-capacity hard disks resident within modern PC housings.

### Floppy disk formats

Floppy disk drives are, in general, a cheap and reliable means of data storage. Two common sizes of drive hardware are currently found on IBM PCs, the first accepting $3\frac{1}{2}''$ floppy disk media, and the second $5\frac{1}{4}''$ disks. Both sizes of disk hardware are found in two formats: *double-density* (DD) and *high-density* (HD). High-density disk drives pack more information

**Table 3.2** IBM PC/MS-DOS disk formats

| Media | Formatted capacity | Comments |
|---|---|---|
| $3\frac{1}{2}''$ DS HD | 1.44Mb | The most common PC disk format. Compact and reliable. Any new machine should be capable of reading HD $3\frac{1}{2}''$ disks. |
| $3\frac{1}{2}''$ DS DD | 720Kb | Can be used reliably in both double density and high density $3\frac{1}{2}''$ disk drives. Thus handy for switching files between new and older machines. Most software is supplied in this format. |
| $5\frac{1}{4}''$ DS HD | 1.2Mb | High-capacity $5\frac{1}{4}''$ format. Once widespread, but now far less common than HD $3\frac{1}{2}''$ disks. Prone to data errors if bent! |
| $5\frac{1}{4}''$ DS DD | 360Kb | Low-capacity $5\frac{1}{4}''$ format. Now only found on older machines. Problems may be experienced reading this type of disk on high density $5\frac{1}{4}''$ drives |

onto a floppy disk, and are almost universal. Any modern PC now purchased should be equipped with a high-density $3\frac{1}{2}''$ disk drive.

Because disk drives come in two sizes and densities, so too do the floppy disk media inserted into the hardware for data storage. Figure 3.3 illustrates (a) $5\frac{1}{4}''$ and (b) $3\frac{1}{2}''$ floppy disk formats. The former consist of a thin magnetic disk within a flexible plastic coating, thus giving rise to the name 'floppy' disk, as $5\frac{1}{4}''$ disks can easily be bent. (This is, however, not advised!) Data is read off a $5\frac{1}{4}''$ floppy disk through a hole in its protective plastic cover. This area of the disk should never touched, and the media should be stored in the supplied paper sleeve at all times.

Just as audio and video tapes have record-protect lugs to prevent the accidental erasure of valuable material, computer disks have *write-protect tabs*. On $5\frac{1}{4}''$ media this consists of a little notch which may be covered with tape to prevent data being erased. Both double and high-density $5\frac{1}{4}''$ disks look identical, except for the wording on the label.

The first thing to note about $3\frac{1}{2}''$ computer disks is that they are not floppy! Instead the magnetic disk on which data is stored is encased in a brittle plastic shell, with a sliding metal screen on one edge allowing the

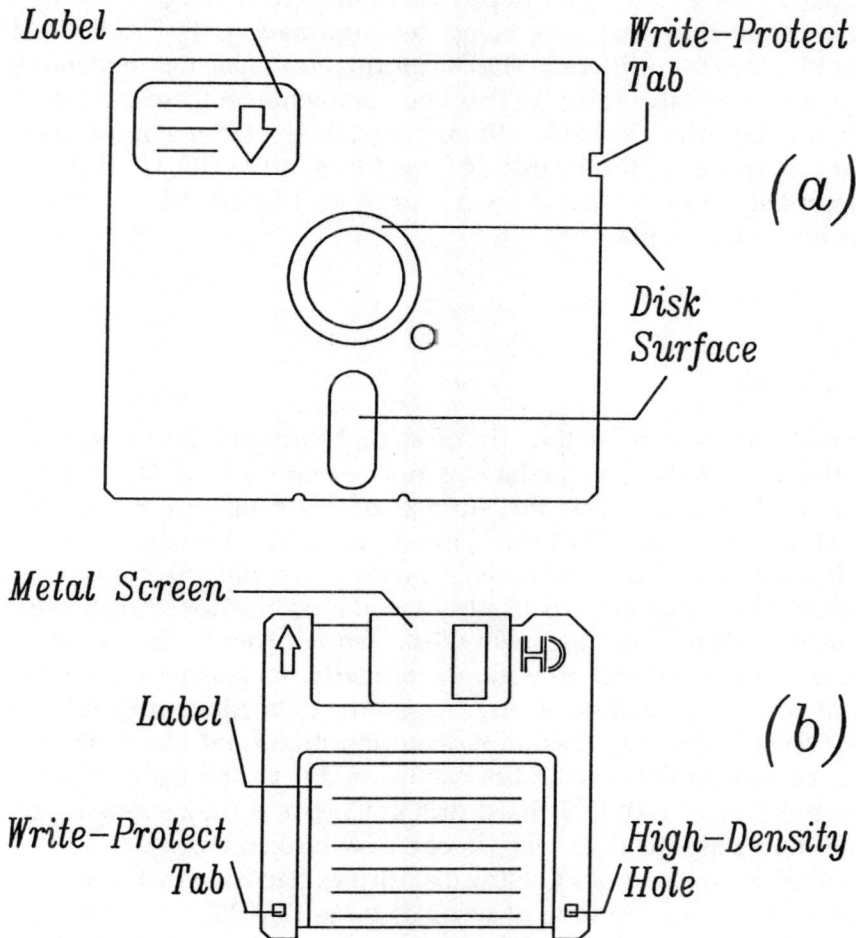

**Figure 3.3**   (a) $5\frac{1}{4}''$ and (b) $3\frac{1}{2}''$ floppy disks

disk drive hardware to access the media surface. A sliding write-protect tab is provided at the disk's bottom left corner. When this tab is left in an 'open' position, data upon the disk cannot be altered. High-density $3\frac{1}{2}''$ disks additionally have the 'HD' insignia top right, as well as an additional square hole bottom right to inform the disk drive hardware of the higher storage capacity. Both the $5\frac{1}{4}''$ and $3\frac{1}{2}''$ disks insert into the computer's disk drive slot in the direction indicated by the arrows as illustrated in figure 3.3.

In chapter 2 we noted that floppy disks need to undergo a 'formatting' process before they can store computer information. $3\frac{1}{2}''$ and $5\frac{1}{4}''$ disks format to one of four different MS-DOS formatted capacities, depending on their size and density. Table 3.2 lists and comments on these formats, all of which use DS (double sided) floppy media. By far the most common formatted capacity is the 1.44Mb obtained from a DS HD $3\frac{1}{2}''$ disk. Future developments in floppy media will shortly lead to 2.88Mb $3\frac{1}{2}''$ disks and drives becoming available.

## Hard disk drives

Hard disk drives may be thought of as high-capacity, high-speed floppy disks from which the data media may not be removed. All PC systems rely on an internal hard disk for storage of their operating system and applications programs. Most users, in addition, also store data files in hard disk directories. It should be noted, however, that data files saved upon a hard disk should *always* be 'backed-up' to at least one floppy disk in case of hard disk failure. For *all* users, disk failure should be regarded as inevitable. **All disks will go wrong eventually**. As a safe rule, it is best to keep at least *three* copies of any important data files on separate data media. Most commonly, this implies storing important files both on your PC's hard disk and on two additional $3\frac{1}{2}''$ or $5\frac{1}{4}''$ floppy disks. Many users ignore this rule – until their hard disk crashes and they suddenly realize that all their precious eggs were in one now-broken basket.

The typical capacity of PC hard disk drives has been increasing almost monthly of late. At the time of writing, some IBM PCs are still supplied with 40Mb hard disk drives, although the norm is for machines with 80 or 105Mb disks. Hard disks of 240Mb are now becoming common in basic desktop PCs. These data capacities may at first seem needlessly huge. A 105Mb hard disk used solely for text storage, for example, could store over 13 million words (equivalent to more than 150 average-sized textbooks). Modern computer software, however, rapidly consumes hard disk space. MS-DOS version 6 and *Microsoft Windows* version 3.1 between them can occupy up to 10Mb of hard disk space, with a modern word processor such as *WordPerfect 6.0* requiring 17Mb for effective operation. PCs with once-standard 40Mb hard disks, simply loaded with DOS, *Windows* and a good word processor and spreadsheet, may have very little room left for user data. Purchasers should thus seek out a PC with the highest capacity hard disk drive they can reasonably afford.

## Removable media

Although traditionally hard disk drives are fixed within the main computer housing, *removable media* hard disk cartridges are now available, which insert into a special hard disk drive. The common capacity for these cartridges is either 44 or 88Mb Whilst initially expensive, by using multiple cartridges, the cost per megabyte for removable media systems falls rapidly. Portable hard disk stores, which can be switched between different PCs, can also be purchased if desired. These are especially useful when large amounts of data need to be shared between different computers, e.g. between home and office PCs.

## CD-ROM storage

**CD-ROM** (compact disk read only memory) drives allow access to huge amounts of data stored on cheap-to-press optical disks. The typical storage capacity of a CD-ROM disk is 600Mb, with data being read by a laser as in audio CD players. Many computer databases are now supplied in CD-ROM format, as are picture libraries and even some forms of software. CD-ROM is also used in **multimedia**, as discussed in chapter 8. The only real problem with CD-ROM drives is the fact that they can only be used for retrieval and not data storage. Other forms of optical disk technology have now been developed, however, which overcome this major limitation.

## WORM drives

A **WORM drive** (standing for write once, read many) is a form of optical disk storage on which data can be stored by the user but never erased. Thus, if a file is replaced on a WORM drive, a copy of the original from which it was derived is still retained. Given the high capacity of these drives (typically 600Mb), this is often not a problem. Indeed, it may be an advantage, allowing easy data audits when searching for the introduction of errors, as files can never be deleted.

## Floptical disks

**Floptical disks** are one of two forms of removable optical media on which data may be both freely written and erased. The drives operate just like normal floppy disks (and at about the same speed), except that $3\frac{1}{2}''$ flopticals have a 20Mb storage capacity. Disk drive hardware designed to access flopticals can also read standard high-density $3\frac{1}{2}''$ disks. A 20Mb floptical disk currently costs around £17.00.

## Magneto-optical disks

A final form of optical disk technology, offering perhaps the ultimate in disk-based storage, allows for fully rewritable media (as with a floptical disk), but with a higher data capacity and the access speed of a hard disk. The technology utilized, as the name suggests, employs both optical and magnetic storage techniques. Specifically, data is written to and read from the disk by a laser, but erased magnetically. **Magneto-optical disks** (frequently referred to just as optical disks) come in both $3\frac{1}{2}''$ and $5\frac{1}{4}''$ sizes, with capacities of either 128, 594 or 650Mb. Price per megabyte is the lowest for any storage media, although the magneto-optical drive hardware required to access the media currently costs far more than the average personal computer.

## PCMCIA cards

Not all computer storage devices are disk based. Others simply rely on RAM chip technology, with their data retained via an inbuilt power cell. The most common storage device of this type is the **PCMCIA card**, a credit-card sized device stuffed with tiny RAM chips and a lithium battery with a life of 1–2 years. Hailed as a significant development, the Personal Computer Memory Card International Association standard and been accepted by most computer manufacturers, implying that many types of computer will be able to access data on PCMCIA cards in the near future.

Storage capacities for PCMCIA cards currently rise to 4Mb, with cards of this capacity currently costing around £120, though the price is expected to fall rapidly once demand exists for high-volume production. Most popular at present on pocket-sized computers and personal organizers, PCMCIA card slots are now starting to appear on desktop personal computers. The cards will also become the storage media for filmless electronic cameras and are used in **personal digital assistants** (PDAs), as discussed in chapter 8.

## Flash RAM

**Flash RAM** storage also relies on memory chips, but of a 'non-volatile' nature. In other words, the memory chips used retain their contents even when the power is removed. The downside of the **EPROM** (erasable programmable read only memory) chips used for flash RAM storage is that their contents can only be erased in bulk (via exposure to a UV flash-tube mounted within the computer). This all-or-nothing erasure technique, whilst highly reliable, is less convenient than that offered by battery-backed PCMCIA cards. As with the latter, flash RAM's predominant current usage is as the storage media on small portable and pocket computers.

## Tape streamers

The final common PC storage device is the **tape streamer**. These are used exclusively to back-up large amounts of data from other storage media (notably hard disks), with the data retained on cartridges of cassette tape. Tape streamer cartridges are available in numerous formats, with capacities up into the gigabytes (thousands of megabytes). Most large organizations regularly tape-stream their computer data, with the cartridges being stored in safe locations (such as fire proof boxes) in case a disaster should befall their computer system.

## A typical office specification

With a brief glance back to figure 3.1, we are now in the position to provide an actual specification for our typical arrangement of desktop hardware (a feat nobody writing about computers should ever attempt!). Piecing together from the above, you should now appreciate that if purchasing an IBM PC or compatible computer today, a minimum specification should comprise the following:

| | |
|---|---|
| Processor | 386-SX or above |
| Clock Speed | 16 MHz or greater |
| Memory | 2Mb RAM or greater |
| Graphics card | VGA or SVGA |
| Hard disk | 80Mb or above |
| Floppy disk drive | HD $3\frac{1}{2}''$ |

## Non-IBM personal computers

Whilst the IBM PC is the most common business hardware 'platform', other manufacturers have managed to acquire sizeable market shares (in terms of numbers of machines sold), in certain niche segments. Three such 'alternative' platforms will be discussed herein, all with remarkable similarities.

Firstly, these three hardware platforms are all based around a range of microprocessors from Motorola, rather than the Intel chip range used in all IBM machines. The most basic processor in the Motorola range is its 68000 chip, with the 68020, 68030 and 68040 CPUs being employed in successively more powerful machines. The three computer ranges below were also all launched in the early-to-mid 1980s with GUIs (graphical user interfaces) as standard. This made them much more user friendly than the CLI (command line interface) based IBM PCs of the period. The final common characteristic of the following systems is that they are all closed architectures. In other words, none of their proprietary manufacturers have allowed alternative hardware makers to supply compatible machines. Whilst in turn inevitably restricting software availability for each machine, the closed architecture approach has meant that build quality and design development have remained consistently high.

## *The Apple Mac*

Famous for its intuitive graphical user interface, Macintosh™ computers established themselves in the DTP market long before *Microsoft Windows* and VGA screen technology emerged for the IBM PC. Although IBM PCs are now capable of matching Apple machines in terms of both hardware and software specification, many people still claim the Mac as the supreme, easy-to-use personal computer for DTP and graphics work.

## *The Commodore Amiga*

Whereas Apple has a stronghold in the DTP sector, the Commodore Amiga range of computers reigns supreme when it comes to desktop video (DTV). The majority of video editing suites are equipped with Amiga personal computers, and many television games shows are dependent on these machines for their graphics. Commodore continues to have difficulty being taken seriously in the business market, as most Amigas sold are still relatively low-specification machines bundled with games and sold without internal hard disks.

## The Atari ST/TT

Atari, like Commodore, first targeted their range of ST and TT computers at the home market, and never gained widespread business acceptance. Atari machines do still dominate one segment of the computer market, due to the fact that they have always been equipped with *MIDI* (musical instrument digital interface) ports allowing computer control of electronic synthesizers. Most musicians therefore work with Atari machines both at home and in the recording studio. This range of computers also offers an excellent, if underexploited, platform for DTP.

## File compatibility

Although none of the above machines will run IBM-compatible programs, it is a fairly straightforard task to transfer data files back and forth between these computers and IBM machines. Intuitively, this has always been obvious: with Apples, Amigas and ST/TTs all possessing $3\frac{1}{2}''$ disk drives, problems of data transfer were inevitably just software-based.

For many years analysts and journalists shunned machines based upon the Motorola chipset as totally and utterly incompatible with anything else at all (even though many enthusiasts were regularly swapping files back and forth). Over the past couple of years, however, the official position has changed drastically. Most significantly, one of Apple Computer's current advertising points is that their machines will now read and write IBM PC formatted MS-DOS disks. You can thus begin writing a document on a PC, save it to disk, and load it back into a Mac to continue your literary creation. Similarly, Commodore Amigas now have MS-DOS disk compatibility offered as standard. Surprisingly, Atari ST/TT machines have *always* read MS-DOS disks directly – even though few people seemed to be aware of the fact, and less still advertised it! The problem of transferring data files – and in particular word-processed documents – between different computer platforms is thus illusionary. There may be some very good reasons for not purchasing a Mac, Amiga or ST/TT, but file compatibility with IBM machines is no longer one of them. If it were, I would not now be scattering text into an Amiga to load back into my office PC tomorrow morning. How ironic it is that a chapter predominantly concerning IBM personal computers has been written on a different hardware platform! Or maybe it just demonstrates how mature the computer hardware market has become.

## Summary

This chapter has provided an overview of the IBM PC, together with a detailed coverage of most forms of computer input, storage and output device. Specifically, it has addressed:

- IBM PC CPU, speed, memory and graphics formats;
- Keyboards, mice and other pointer devices;
- Scanners and digitizers;
- Monitors and other display hardware;
- Computer printers;
- Floppy and hard disk formats and capacities;
- Optical disks and non-disk storage media; and
- Alternative PC platforms.

## Review exercise

The following three IBM PCs are all advertised cheaply in your local paper. Explain the merits and drawbacks of each system.

1. 16 MHz 286 PC, EGA graphics, 2Mb RAM, 105Mb hard disk, $3\frac{1}{2}''$ DD DD and $5\frac{1}{4}''$ DS HD floppy disk drives.
2. 33 MHz 386-DX PC, SVGA graphics, 1Mb RAM, 40Mb hard disk, $5\frac{1}{4}''$ DS HD floppy disk drive.
3. 20 MHz 486-SX PC, VGA graphics, 2Mb RAM, 80Mb hard disk, $5\frac{1}{4}''$ DS HD $3\frac{1}{2}''$ floppy disk drive.

Which of the above would you recommend for purchase and why? What hardware devices would you also recommend for additional purchase?

# 4 Communications and network architecture

In the 1980s personal computers proliferated like a plague of rabbits across the workplace, allowing individuals to run their own, discrete applications. The 1990s, however, is already the decade of widespread PC interconnection, with hitherto isolated users communicating electronically to share both data and applications resources. This chapter explores personal computer communications, arrangements for their interconnection across 'networks', and the distinction between 'client–server' and 'peer-to-peer' network systems.

## Getting technical

Any discussion concerning computer interconnection has a tendency to become swamped in detailed hardware specifics. This chapter, although adopting a conceptual approach, is therefore the most technically complex within this *Blueprint*. For managers involved with IT systems it also is one of the most important. Many users have initial reservations when 'their' PCs are connected to others, almost as if a very personal domain is being invaded. The progression from stand-alone to networked PCs, however, is as inevitable as the evolution from typewriter and sliderule to personal computer. Any organization that shies away from network installation will thus get as rapidly antiquated as the one that decided not to introduce computers in the first place.

## Communications, networks and distributed processing

At a basic level, communications facilities allow computers resident in different locations to exchange data and/or program resources. And every time two or more computers are connected for exchange purposes they are said to comprise a *network*. New hardware and software technologies are now making computer communications more rapid and reliable than in the past, and hence networks of personal and other computers are becoming more commonplace. It is worth remembering, however, that the practice of accessing a computer resource remote from the user is not a recent one.

Until the rise of the microcomputer, almost all business users accessed mainframe or minicomputer systems via dumb terminal devices. Such *teleprocessing* relied on all processing operations taking place centrally. The widespread adoption and interconnection of personal computers has now made *distributed processing* possible, with both the user base and the majority of processing hardware being remote from the centre. Reliance on central systems has therefore diminished, with distributed processing across a range of interconnected machines being a key driving force towards the downsizing of computer operations.

The whole area of computer interconnection is vast. In particular, the term 'network' now covers a multitude of computer communication and resource-distribution patterns and technologies. It is thus wise to consider the basic means of computer communication before entering into a specific exploration of network systems.

## Computer communications

All communications media are based around a sending device, a communications link and some form of receiver. In the case of computer communications, both the sending and receiving devices will be some category of personal, mini or mainframe computer. Attention is thus largely focused on the type of communications link adopted to connect the computers in question.

Technically, connecting computers together (especially over long distances) can be a complex and troublesome proposition. Most notably, problems abound with conflicting standards, inadequate data transmission speeds and hardware expense. The physical components that comprise any computer-to-computer link (e.g. connectors, interfaces and wiring), are also much more prone to failure than the machines they bring together (Trimmer, 1993: 162). With the inherently technical and oft enigmatic nature of computer communications in mind, many in business opt for blissful ignorance of technologies, problems and solutions. It is surely more sensible, however, to place acquaintance with potentially troublesome arenas higher on your agenda than other concerns. Business computer users are hence encouraged to obtain a broad understanding of computer communications to avoid being sandbagged into solutions derived in the best interests of technicians, but perhaps not the organization as a whole.

## Communication links

There are a great many ways of linking computers together. Data may, for example, be communicated over public telephone lines, various forms of in-situ electrical cabling, optical fibres, microwave relays or even satellite link-ups. All but the first of these technologies needs to be dedicated to the communications link in question, their closed (or private) nature inevitably constraining the breadth of user interconnection. Utilizing telephone lines, on the other hand, allows open access to the international telecommunications network and hence the widest range of link possibilities for computer-to-computer communication.

## Modems and telephone communication

To communicate via the public telephone system, a personal computer needs to be connected to a piece of hardware known as a **modem**. This device serves as the interface between the computer and the telephone socket, translating digital communications signals derived from the computer into analogue waveforms that can pass down telephone lines. The process of converting digital computer information into wave-based analogue signals is called *modulation*. The reverse process (translating analogue signals back into a digital form) is known as *demodulation*. A modem thus gets its name from the combination of these terms, being a data signal modulator/demodulator.

Computer modems come in two forms: *direct connect* and *acoustic coupler*. Direct connect modems are most common in the office, comprising internal interface cards or small external adaptors that plug into a PC and then directly into a telephone socket. Acoustic coupler modems, on the other hand, connect the computer to a telephone receiver by the placement of the handset in a special bay. They are thus less convenient (and more prone to error) than direct connection devices, but carry the advantage of being able to be connected to any telephone. Acoustic coupler modems are thus very useful for portable computer users who may wish to connect to office machines from many locations, including public telephone boxes.

Figure 4.1 illustrates the interconnection of hardware for a telecommunications link between two personal computers. With the replacement of one of the PCs with a larger machine, the figure could just as easily

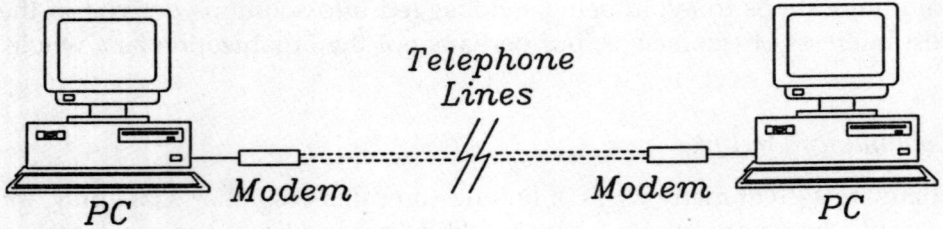

**Figure 4.1** Modem communications

represent the communications chain between a mainframe or mini-computer and a desktop machine. Modem use is predicted to increase as portable computing on the move becomes more widespread, and pocket-sized radio telephones proliferate. Combination portable telephone and computer devices are also predicted to appear. Telephone exchanges in the twenty-first century are therefore just as likely to be connecting machines for digital parlance as they are to be bringing together their owners for organic conversation. Fortunately, a largely unheralded overhaul of the telephone system is now nearing completion to cope with the expected increase in both mobile and computer-generated traffic.

*Modem specifics*

Modern modems come equipped with a range of user-friendly features. A minimum specification should include *auto-answering* of incoming calls and *auto-disconnect* to hang-up automatically at the end of a communication. Software to automate the dialling process (*auto-dial*) is also extremely useful. The most common standard for modems is *Hayes compatible*, featuring auto answering, disconnect and dialling, together with a host of other functions.

Finally, it should be noted that modems come in a range of data transmission speeds. Early devices transmitted data at only 100 or 300 bits per second (*bps*) – one *bit* of information being equivalent to one-eighth of a byte. Modern hardware typically offers transmission speeds of 1200, 2400, 9600, 14,00 or even 19,200 bps. Purchasers should clearly seek to obtain modems that will operate at the highest possible transmission speeds, in order to save on both time and telephone charges. For data transmission at speeds exceeding 19,200 bps, public telephone lines become technically inadequate and users must turn to dedicated computer linkages.

## Dedicated computer links

As already noted, there are a great many link technologies for computer interconnection. The public telecommunications network provides a widespread and easy to access medium, but it cannot offer high-speed data transmission or be considered secure for sensitive communications. Depending on the distances involved, organizations may thus turn to one or a combination of the following forms of computer link-up:

- private/leased telephone lines (including ISDN);
- satellite or microwave transmissions; and
- wire-pairs or coaxial cables.

When companies decide to invest in dedicated telecommunications links, either purchased or more commonly hired from a telecommunications operator, they may well opt for an **ISDN** (Integrated Services Digital Network) line. These provide high-speed channels for both voice, video and data communications, and frequently utilize fibre-optic strands rather than electrical cabling to increase carrier capacity.

Also used for dedicated computer communications across long distances are both satellite and microwave transmission systems. Geostationary communications satellites are still being launched to provide transmission pathways for financially endowed communicators wanting the best in international link-ups. Microwave data transmission systems are more common than satellite links, being employed for communications over relatively short land distances. As they transmit through the atmosphere, microwave systems must have their dishes in a direct 'line-of-sight' of no more than 30 miles, although relay stations may be constructed to boost communications over longer distances.

Within an office, building or complex such as a university campus, dedicated direct wiring is usually employed as the interconnection medium for computer systems. This takes the form of either **wire-pair** or **coaxial** cabling. Wire pairs (sometimes known as **twisted pairs**), consist of individual wires twisted together within an insulated cable. Their use in computer connection is common because they have often been installed in a building for other purposes, such as telephone or security system interconnection. Unfortunately, wire-pairs are susceptible to electrical interference from high-voltage electrical cabling, which in turn may corrupt data signals transmitted down these wires. Wiring-pair systems can also only be used for relatively short communications distances of up to about 100 metres.

Coaxial cables offer a higher quality and more rapid means of data transmission than twisted-pair wiring links. Here a central wire is enclosed within a circular earth shield, reducing the chance of electrical interference. Many people will recognize coaxial cables from their use in television, video and high-quality audio connection leads. Data may be transmitted further by coaxial cabling than by twisted-pair wiring (with runs of up to 500 metres being permissible), and although expensive to install, this form of computer interconnection is increasingly common.

## Computer networks

### Black arts and jargon clans

There are two breeds of user in many offices: those who understand the principles of the network, and those who are amazed that it works at all. Of all the now-widespread computer knowledge arenas (IBM PC specification, software classifications, printer technologies and so forth), networking is still by far the most mystical. Perhaps this is because it is also the most recent, and debatably the most powerful. Clans in the know thus copiously protect the lexicon of network operations. As ventured in the pages of a respected computer magazine: 'Over the years the technicians of the industry have turned networking into a Black Art masked in jargon and protected within the inner sanctum of the centralised mainframe or minicomputer department' (Doyle, 1992: 286).

With the mid-1990s fast approaching, the mists surrounding the networking religion will surely begin to disperse. As with many other major changes in computer usage, the driving factor to quell the fog has been the entry of the PC into the arena. Inexpensive networks of personal computers are now commonplace, and may be effectively implemented across relatively small clusters of users. In turn, a familiarity with network usage is becoming more widespread, opening eyes to broader potentials for computer connectivity.

### WANs and LANs

When computers are connected either to exchange data or share program resources, the species of network so conceived is contingent upon the distance between the machines in question. For communications over large distances, there is the **wide area network** (WAN). For smaller distance interconnection and resource sharing, there is the **local area network**

(LAN). Most large organizations will operate WANs to interconnect their computers systems across different locations, as well as LANs to allow computer communication within sites, buildings or offices. Most LAN facilities will therefore be configured with connection *gateways* into company WANs to allow their users to engage in non-local communication. Any computer or dumb terminal device connected to a network may be referred to as a network *node*.

## Wide area networks

Because of the distances involved, most WANs use either public or dedicated telecommunications lines for their communications links. They are also likely to be based around either a mini or mainframe 'host' computer, with which most users will communicate via a dumb terminal. Personal computers, however, can also be connected to a WAN (usually via a modem) to access central data files. When a PC user needs to run applications programs only available via a WAN, they will probably have to execute *terminal emulation software*. This program genre effectively makes any PC behave like a dumb terminal console with no native processing capacity. Indeed terminal emulation programs may be regarded as evolving PCs back one stage, in order to function as mere input–output appendages connected to mainframe or minicomputer based systems.

## Local area networks

Local area networks are now common in PC-inhabited buildings and offices. Because of the short distances involved, they usually rely on either twisted-pair or coaxial cabling as their means of machine interconnection. This said, wireless LAN systems are being developed, as are **FDDI**s (fibre distributed data interfaces) to allow rapid and long-distance LAN communications over fibre-optic strands rather than electrical wires.

To gain access to a LAN, a PC must be fitted with a piece of hardware known as a *network interface card*. This provides the machine with a socket for connection to the network wiring. Network software also needs to be installed, allowing transmission to, and reception from, other computers on the network. One of the most common PC network packages is called *Novell Netware*, with about 60 per cent of the PC LAN software market share.

*LAN facilities*

LAN interconnection for the PC user brings with it many advantages. The three key benefits bestowed by LAN interconnection are:

- common storage access;
- common peripheral access; and
- common software access.

The LAN facility for common storage access will enable all users to store and retrieve data from either a central data store or each other's hard disk drives. Data duplication is thus curtailed, and all users can always be working with the latest, up-to-date version of a file. Many PC LANs feature a host or **server** computer to control the system. A server is effectively just a powerful computer with a very large hard disk (perhaps 1 gigabyte in capacity), which may be accessed for data storage and retrieval by each PC on the LAN. To many users, LAN connection simply means having access to a very large, commonly accessible hard disk drive.

The benefit of common peripheral access is another reason for connecting office PCs into a LAN. The peripherals most likely to be shared are hardcopy devices, especially expensive printers like lasers. Every PC on a network, for example, will be able to direct output to the same laser printer or plotter, thus reducing the expenditure required on frequently idle output hardware.

Common software access across a LAN allows all users to access the same applications programs, which are usually installed on the central server computer. Licenses for network software that may be accessed by many users work out cheaper than buying individual program copies for each PC in the office. They also make the upgrading of software a much more straightforward process, as only one copy of the program (on the server) has to be changed, rather than every copy on each stand-alone PC. Having software packages stored on a server (rather than on individual PCs) also saves on hard disk storage capacity, as each PC on the network is not holding a duplicate cope of each application program.

On the down side, there are a few drawbacks associated with network operations. Although in theory LAN connection will have no negative impact on individual PC operations, the network software required will eat up some precious RAM and hard disk space. There may also be some problems getting certain pieces of software to run over a LAN, although these can usually be overcome. Finally, LAN dependence is a rapid addiction, meaning that when maintenance and failure downtimes occur, staff appear helpless and are often totally unproductive.

## LAN topologies

Personal computers may be inter connected into a LAN configuration in a variety of ways. Three logical shapes or *topology* of local area network are most common, as illustrated in figure 4.2.

A *star network* is arranged with a server computer at its centre, with each individual PC wired in via a separate cable strand (usually a twisted-pair). Because star networks effectively have PCs on individual wheel spokes around their centre, they are sometimes also referred to as *network hubs*. Star topology is the oldest configuration of computer connection, reminiscent of the linkage system between early mainframes and their dumb terminal servants. In a star network, all communications are clearly routed through the central server, thus if it breaks down no machine-to-machine communications are possible.

A *ring network*, as the name implies, has all computers on the network daisy-chained in a circle, with the output of each machine being connected to the input of the next. The system may thus be operated without a server, with each computer being responsible for some network management tasks. The inconvenience of this topology is in having to have the first and last machines in the network physically close enough to close the ring. The advantage, on the other hand, is that even if the network ring is broken in one place, data transfer between nodes can still take place. The most common LAN of this type is the **Token Ring**™ system from IBM.

Finally, *bus networks* are now the most widespread business LAN topology, with all PC nodes and the server being connected to a common bus line (most frequently a coaxial cable). Each PC has some resident software for network management, and hence if the server fails, PC-to-PC communications are (in theory!) still possible. Bus systems are effectively open rings, and thus will fail if a single link is broken between machines. Probably the most common form of bus network connection system is **ethernet**, which uses a coaxial cable as the common line to which all machines are connected. Ethernet networks may be recognized in offices by the existence of wall boxes with two protruding video-style BNC sockets offering a link into the main bus cable. Because a bus network line must not be broken, small link cables are fitted to ethernet boxes if the socket is not in use, and should never be removed.

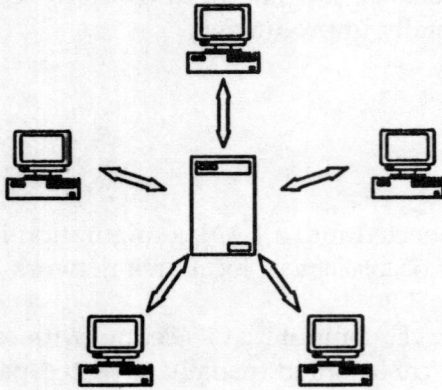

*Star Network*

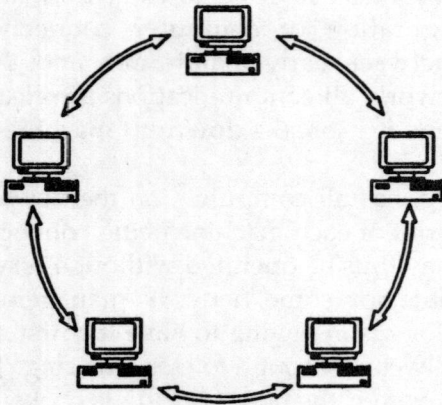

*Ring Network*

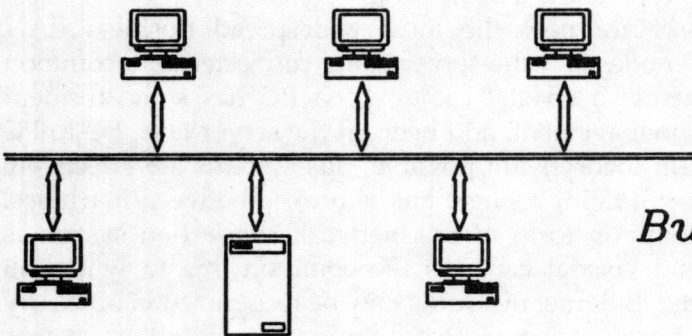

*Bus Network*

**Figure 4.2**   LAN topologies

## Alternative network architectures

One of the main threads of the downsizing movement, as explored by proponent Dan Trimmer (1993), has been the rapid development of so called **client–server architectures**. This type of computer system is being increasingly referred to in popular management and information technology literatures. It is also reported to be one of the most rapidly developing areas of business computing. Thus, whilst essentially involving the same concepts as explored above, client–server and alternative systems are also worth noting separately.

### *Client–server systems*

Client–server architectures imply an interconnected system wherein two complementary types of computer have been designed to work in conjunction with each other. One of these computer types will exist to serve the resource needs of the other type, and is thus referred to as the *server*. All other computers, of the second type, will operate as *clients* of the former, utilizing the facilities of the server machine.

Typical client–server configurations include PC-to-PC based LANs, with one high-specification IBM PC working to serve lower-specification PCs as its clients. Alternatively, minicomputer-to-PC client–server systems will have a minicomputer host (such as an IBM AS/400) providing server facilities to a range of PCs. Client-server architectures may also exist with minicomputer-to-minicomputer network links.

Whatever type of machine is chosen to fill the client and server roles, the critical notion of client–server is that both machine types involved possess native processing capacity (unlike dumb terminals in mainframe-to-terminal computer systems). Client machines are therefore provided with *additional* network services by their server, rather than having a total operations interdependence with the more powerful host computer.

### *Peer-to-peer architecture*

Most personal computer networks are client–server based, with one large host computer (the server) running the show for dozens of PC clients. Server computers, however, can be expensive both to purchase and maintain. Thus when only a small LAN is needed (perhaps simply to allow printer sharing between a handful of users in a small office), **peer-to-peer** systems are often invoked. This architecture type is not based around a server (thus saving on hardware expense), and instead allows all computers in the arrangement to share each other's resources. Within a peer-to-peer PC network, all users may have file access to each other's hard disk drive in order to share both programs and data. They will also be able to access any peripheral attached to any machine. Expensive peripherals like laser printers may thus be purchased singly and shared by all network users even when connected to just one PC.

Typical peer-to-peer technology is suited to networks of perhaps four or five PCs running a few MS-DOS or *Microsoft Windows* based applications. Systems can be installed and up-and-running in a matter of hours (if not minutes!), with no complex installation procedures to endure as common with client–server system initiations (Goodwins, 1992). Peer-to-peer architectures are much slower than client–server system equivalents, with no server computer optimized for file access and communications operations. Proper system security is also a must, with the designation of one user as a *system manager* charged with restricting disk access being crucial for non-argumentative peer-to-peer operations. Few people would be happy if another user inadvertently deleted files off *their* hard disk without permission! Carefully managed by sensible people, peer-to-peer systems may bring significant networking advantages to small user groups to whom the expense of a server-based architecture would prove prohibitive.

## Communications services and applications

In addition to common storage, common peripheral and common software access, most forms of computer interconnection bring with them a whole spectrum of potential new communications services and/or applications. By far the most common new application resulting from the birth of computer networks has to be electronic mail.

### Electronic mail

Electronic mail systems allow network users to communicate messages electronically from one computer to another. Rather than having memos typed and photocopied, they can simply be keyed to the screen and distributed to as many users on the network as required. E-mail systems not only save on paper (and the desk space consumed by the same), but also bring messages more immediately to the attention of their recipient. A sender can also be assured that their message has not gone astray. Many software packages now exist to allow e-mail to be transmitted across PC LANs, e.g. *Pegasus Mail*™. For wider e-mail communications, electronic mail boxes may be leased from service bureau or messages routed via public data services such as *CompuServe*.

Internal e-mail systems do, of course, assume that users will turn on their computers and *login* to check their electronic mail boxes on a frequent basis. They can also increase an already abundant stream of perhaps unnecessary internal communication within an organization, as e-mail messages are so easy to send and reply to, and may be directed to many recipients simultaneously.

## On-line databases

Once a computer is equipped for communications, users will probably find no difficulty in locating a range of *on-line database services* they may wish to access. On-line databases are effectively large information stores which may accessed by computer and used to research topics via selective questioning. Useful information is then *downloaded* back to your own computer. Most services of this nature, such as *DataStream*, which contains a wealth of company financial statistics, charge a registration fee to access their service, coupled with a charge based on the call-time for information obtained. Used effectively, an on-line database can be a very cost-effective research tool. Used ineffectively, they can cost a small fortune.

## Bulletin boards

**Bulletin boards** are an interactive service allowing their subscribers both to read and post messages. Boards usually specialize in certain topics or interests, with subscribers exchanging information on a myriad of subjects as diverse as computer purchasing, sport, politics, art and romance. **Public domain** (PD) software may also be downloaded from a bulletin board, distributed free by authors who create PD programs for their own pleasure.

## Electronic funds transfers

Many organizations are now equipped for electronic banking and EFTs (electronic funds transfers) via computer network links. Most people use

EFT systems without realizing it every time they use a cashpoint or a direct debit card in a shop. Fund transfers by computers greatly reduce banking costs, and offer potentially increased security safeguards.

## Packet switch stream systems

With all the above and more data services now being available via computer network linkages, the potential to run up very high telephone or line rental charges is high. Fortunately **packet switch stream** (PSS) communications systems have been developed to minimize data transmission costs. PSS systems effectively allow for national and international connections at near local prices, with users using conventional telephone lines to access their local PSS *node*. From this point, once a charging code has been entered, national and international connections are made within the PSS system at well below normal telecommunications rates.

## Summary

This last chapter of part I has provided a broad, relatively non-technical overview of both the means of, and arrangements for, computer interconnection and communication. Specifically chapter 4 has addressed:

- modem communications;
- dedicated computer links;
- wide and local area networks (WANs and LANs);
- LAN facilities and topologies;
- Client–server and peer-to-peer architectures; and
- E-mail and communications services.

## Discussion questions

1. How do you come into contact with computer telecommunication services in your daily life?
2. What additional computer-based communications or network facilities would you like to have available?

# PART II
# Management and computer application

# 5 Management and information systems

In chapter 1 we noted that computers are simply information processing tools. It therefore comes as no surprise that they play a pivotal role in the information systems of most organizations. Indeed, the term **IS** (information system) has become synonymous with any computer-based data processing or analysis procedure or installation. This chapter looks at the nature of management, information and systems as a prelude to an examination of the type of information system options now available. The role of IS in achieving corporate 'excellence' is also discussed, together with an exploration of current trends and concerns in IS strategy.

## Management, information and systems

Both managers and computer systems are charged with processing large quantities of information – stock levels, production quotas, sales figures, credit balances, salaries, profits, losses, taxes, insurance contributions, marketing projections, strategic plans and even the weekly expenditure on coffee. The list of data sources and information requirements in modern business is both daunting and apparently endless. The more we inform, the more others wish to know, and the more bureaucratic scrutiny we come under from agencies employed to check we are informing them correctly. And so information processing spirals to new and dizzier heights, the more organizations need to expend on coffee, and the longer their staff spend lying awake at night worrying about it all. Thank goodness that, in the midst of colossal information overkill, modern managers can turn to information systems for assistance – even if the infernal computers on which they are centred did fuel the information revolution in the first place.

With the increased complexity of modern business and organizations, and near-stagnant employee productivity levels in many industries, few analysts would dispute that computer-based information systems have become a critical component in many organizations: 'Most firms nowadays depend on IT for routine operational procedures, and for some firms IT is also important in gaining strategic advantage' (Buck-Lew et al., 1992: 69). Indeed, computers are now embedded in most large administrative systems to such an extent that the technology's removal would prove nigh-on impossible. Similarly, many business activities are inexorably intertwined with information technology. The study of information systems has therefore come to rank alongside finance, marketing, strategic management and other key business disciplines. In particular the role of *management information systems* has become a popular area of concern. To comprehend why information systems have become so important, and also their inherent limitations, is it perhaps best to step back and consider the nature of management, the nature of information, and the nature of systems.

## The nature of management

Classical management scientists such as Henri Fayol (1949) and F. W. Taylor (1947) defined management by listing its involved key *functions*. These included planning, deciding, controlling, monitoring and sanctioning. Normative theories were therefore produced, with the management process clearly specified within a range of scientific rules or *principles*. If embraced in this fashion, management may clearly benefit from the assistance of computer systems in the automation of its functional processes.

More recent management gurus have focused on how successful managers actually spend their time. Mintzberg (1973), for example, suggests that managers fulfil a variety of *roles*, or 'organized sets of behaviours identified with a position'. Three key role sets are noted by Mintzberg, subdivided as follows:

- Interpersonal roles:
  - figurehead;
  - leader;
  - liaison.
- Informational roles:
  - monitor;
  - disseminator;
  - spokesperson.
- Decisional roles:
  - entrepreneur;
  - disturbance handler;
  - resource allocator;
  - negotiator.

The key tasks of a manager may therefore be seen to encompass the work design of an organization, the monitoring of its internal and external environment, the initiation of change when necessary, and the renewal of stability when faced with disturbance (Dobson and Starkey, 1993: 140). Handy (1993: 322) succinctly encapsulates these role tasks, stating that a manager's role is to lead, administrate and fix!

Whilst computer-based information systems may aid a manager in the accomplishment of all the above role chores, they will be most beneficial in the automation and *augmentation* (assistance) of informational and decisional task activities. In other words, computers may help to administer and fix the organization, but will be of little value in providing leadership, strategy and direction. This important point may seem obvious, but does highlight the fact that however complex management information and other computer systems become, they will never replace human employees due to the broad range of managerial roles to be fulfilled.

## The nature of information

> Reliable information is crucial to making projections and anticipating events.   (Stock, 1993: 66)

But what is information? In a strictly technical sense, information is data that has been processed into a useful form. Data may be viewed as an abundant raw material with which both humans and organizations are continually bombarded. No human entity or organization can possible cope with all the data it receives, and thus must employ a filtering process to select valued items. All data selected as worthy of further attention evolves into information. Managers and organizations therefore need to be aware of the qualities of 'good' information in order to employ an effective data selection process. In particular, information will ideally be:

- relevant;
- accurate;
- concise;
- timely;
- well presented;
- complete;
- up to date; and
- cost effective.

Computer systems can clearly aid organizations in the processing of data into accurate, well-presented, up-to-date and cost-effective information. Whether that information is also concise, relevant, timely and complete will be largely contingent upon the capabilities of the people involved in its processing and selection. Therefore, just as information technology may help a manager to administrate and fix but not to lead, so it may aid in the attainment of certain key information properties but not others.

It should also be noted that within organizations information will exist in two forms: *formal* and *informal*. Formal information will be derived from specific operational and business data sources – e.g. the latest output and sales figures. This will then be communicated through recognized channels and treated as hard fact. Informal information, on the other hand, is much softer in nature – e.g. gossip, hearsay and speculation, as passed by word of mouth through the grapevine. Informal information may pertain, however, to critical issues such as industrial unrest or potential problems with customer and supplier relations.

Effective managers seem to cherish 'soft' information: today's gossip frequently becomes tomorrow's fact (Mintzberg, 1975: 228). Any computer-based information system, of course, will only present managers with formal information. A total reliance on information systems is therefore not only impractical but dangerous. Meetings in the corridor, in the canteen and on the golf course can have just as great an impact on a manager's decision making as their scrutiny of the latest profit and loss figures as encapsulated in an MIS report. Once again, we see that computer systems can only encroach so far into the manager's task domain.

## The nature of systems

A system is defined as a set of interacting, interdependent parts which together comprise a unitary whole that performs some function. Key to this definition are the concepts of interaction, interdependence and functionality. A pile of automobile components does not constitute a system. When connected together to a form a working engine, however, the parts become interdependent and interact in the production of locomotive force, and may therefore be viewed as a system conglomeration. In a similar vein, PC hardware needs to be purposefully interconnected and under software manipulation to perform system functions.

The analysis of systems, the subsystems parts of which most are comprised, and the environments in which most exist, comes under the banner of *general systems theory* (GST). GST first originated in biology, and its axioms are usually attributed to Bertalanffy (1951).

In an organizational context, systems theory is directed towards a study of the global work processes of an organization, the tasks of its parts (or divisions), and the relationships, interdependencies and communications linkages between them. Systems theory is becoming increasingly applicable in organizational analysis due to the emergence of organic network structures, with clearly bounded autonomous subsystem nodes interacting with a central, coordinating core (Barnatt, 1992: 513).

By studying organizations as conglomerations of interacting, interdependent subsystems, managers and analysts can cut across the disciplines of management and information science to isolate coherent business solutions. For example, different computer systems (such as PC LANs for accounts, stock control and personnel) may be thought of as subsystems of an organizational information system. This global information system can then in turn be viewed as one of the many interacting components constituting the entire organization. Analysing organizations as systems emphasizes the fact that any information system installation must be seen as one part of the whole organization, and not just as an aspect of the IT department.

## Defining information systems

Having briefly appraised the nature of management, information and systems, we are in a position to consider the basic characteristics of any 'information system'. Clearly such systems will exist to aid information processing within organizations, and (being systems) will include several interdependent, interacting components. By common inference, they will also involve the use of computer systems (or in other words information technology). With an umbrella discipline as callow as IS, any delineation of *exactly* what is included may be difficult to precisely define (Edwards et al., 1991: 6). A general definition is, however, of some analytical value, and herein an information system will be regarded as any 'combination of work practices, information, people, and information technologies organized to accomplish goals in an organization' (Alter, 1992: 7).

It can at once be noted that information systems are generally viewed as amalgams of computers *and* human employees. They are *not* simply concerned with information technology. Computers, after all, are simply tools created by humans to further their endeavours, and thus will complement rather than replace human effort within any system in which

**Table 5.1** Work characteristics: human beings versus computer systems

| Variable | Human beings | Computer systems | Comparative advantage |
|---|---|---|---|
| Running costs | high | low | computers |
| Overhead expenditure | high | low | computers |
| Information processing capacity | low | high | computers |
| Information processing capability | low | high | computers |
| Information processing accuracy | low | high | computers |
| Performance over time | variable | constant | ??? |
| Language abilities | high | low | human |
| Capability to cope with the unexpected | high | nil | humans |
| Ability to plan, compromise and negotiate | high | nil | humans |
| Comprehension level | high | nil | humans |
| Common sense level | high | nil | humans |

they are utilized. A key IS question therefore concerns the nature of the task divide between human employees and computer systems. A second IS debate relates to the impact of computer technology on human working practices. Indeed, many of the problems inherent in effective IS operation occur at the human-computer interface, and are discussed in depth in chapter 6.

## The role of computers

The widely differing work characteristics of human beings and computer systems, whilst leading to problems with their harmonious integration, also render each comparative advantage in certain areas of activity. Table 5.1 details the deviation between human worker and computer system performance across a range of key business variables.

Due to the distinct comparative advantages of computer systems over human workers as illustrated at the top of the table, computers are generally employed in three distinct roles:

- to improve cost-effectiveness;
- to increase business growth potential; and
- to automate or augment decision making.

## Improving cost-effectiveness

The use of computer systems to improve cost-effectiveness is clear to most people within organizations today. Printing cheques or standard letters, totalling balance sheets or searching though data files – in all these and more computers enjoy absolute cost advantages when medium or large throughput volumes are required. Problems may abound with worker relations, trade unions and structural unemployment, but where processing-intensive, zero-creativity office tasks are the order of the day, computers reign supreme in terms of pure economics.

## Increasing business growth

When it comes to increasing business growth potential, the benefit of employing computer systems is perhaps less apparent. Here advantage in computer utilization stems from the fact that the growth of many organizations (or functions thereof) can be constrained by their human administrative systems. Constraints that may be eased via computerization.

Consider, for example, invoice or payroll processing. To process 200 invoices or payroll slips by hand will take approximately twice as long (and therefore cost twice as much) as processing 100 items. This will not be the case for a computer system, with most of its costs being incurred during process initiation activities (such as threading the printer with the appropriate forms and running the required applications software). A computer system may therefore process 200 invoice or payroll slips with perhaps only 10 per cent more time and cost incurrance than when processing 100 forms. Administrative constraints on business growth may therefore be considerably eased via IS implementation, allowing companies to deal with increased throughput volumes whilst enjoying decreased per-unit overhead costs.

## Aiding the decision process

There are two categories of decision: *programmable* and *non-programmable*. Programmable decisions involve no creative input and can be encapsulated in fixed rules or procedures. Computers may therefore be employed to automate the making of programmable decisions. A common example is found in stock control systems, with computers often programmed to automatically place new orders once supplies fall below a certain level. A second example may be found within the environmental control systems of intelligent buildings, with the windows opening automatically once the internal temperature rises above a predetermined threshold. In the home, central heating controllers may be viewed as IS components charged with the mundane exercise of when to turn the hot water boiler on and off.

Entrusting programmable decision making to computer systems enables managers to concentrate on more speculative and complex non-programmable decisions. These tend to involve a creative component, with each decision being one-of-a-kind. Thus, although past lessons may be utilized in selecting courses of action, they will never be able to fully guide judgement. A non-programmable decision, for example, may involve deciding upon the retail price and wrapper colour for a new chocolate bar. Here a computer may be used to process and present information on sales revenues at various price levels, and could statistically project figures for likely sales in different price bands. It could also illustrate the chocolate bar wrapper on-screen in various hues, and perhaps even suggest the colour the public would find most attractive based upon past sales data. Ultimately, however, the decision on price and wrapper colour would have to be taken by one or more human beings. Computers may speed their judgement via the rapid processing of sales and cost data into quality decision information, but the technology's role would of necessity be augmentative.

## Information system classifications

The different roles that may be played by computers within an organization have lead to the evolution of a family of interrelated information systems. Five IS species are typically isolated:

- data processing systems;
- management information systems;
- decision support systems;
- executive information systems; and
- office automation systems.

## Data processing systems

**Data processing** (DP) involves IS at its lowest level. Here technology is integrated into organizational working practices simply to automate tasks more cost-effectively undertaken by computer systems. Common examples include cheque processing, funds transfer, accounts administration, travel reservation, hotel booking, pension administration and personnel record systems. Because their role is usually to aid in the collection, storage and retrieval of information transactions, data processing systems may also be referred to as *transaction processing systems*.

## Management information systems

Once a DP system is in operation, the utilization of the data it contains to aid management control and organizational coordination becomes a logical step forward. A ***management information system*** (MIS) is simply a data processing system with additional facilities allowing management to extract summarized information. This information will allow managers to keep up to date with organizational performance versus goal expectations. A MIS may therefore be used both as a control and a decision aid.

A supermarket MIS, for example, will probably be linked into a store's barcode-scanning checkouts. The system may thus allow the store manager to assess the efficiency of each checkout operator by providing figures on the number of items or perhaps even the goods value passing though each sales point per hour. The system may also provide continuously updated sales figures on every product line, or perhaps even different areas of the store. Managers will therefore be in a position to review accurately the success of sales campaigns or other marketing innovations.

In a similar vein, many companies employing a large number of VDU operators for high-volume data keying employ MIS systems that monitor operator keystrokes per hour as a measure of worker efficiency. Some, like British Telecom, have even linked bonus payment to keystrokes-per-hour figures, although this can pressure operators and lead to long-term occupational health risks (Wood, 1992: 105).

## Decision support systems

The role of computers in making both programmable and non-programmable decisions has already been discussed. A **decision support system** (DSS) commonly refers to a management information system with additional data analysis and modelling features specifically designed to assist in the decision process. The term DSS, however, encompasses a great many software variants, from MIS descended systems to desktop spreadsheets to heuristically based *expert systems*, as discussed in chapter 8.

Decision support systems may aid both the automation of repetitive, routine decisions, and the augmentation of non-programmable decisions. Many insurance agents, for example, apply a structured DSS to help their clients choose their preferred policy option (Alter, 1992: 135). Such systems simply require the input of details concerning age, salary, medical history and occupation, from which the most suitable policies available can be computed. It is even predicted that electronic shopping systems will soon be with us offering customers decision support. Users will simply have to insert a card into a shopping terminal with a touch-sensitive screen, which will then call up a regular shopping list based upon previous purchasing decisions (Bird, 1993b: 83).

Perhaps more usefully in management application, a DSS usually allows a common framework and set of modelling tools to be utilized for decisions of the non-programmable genre. 'What-if?' analysis, for example, is a common DSS feature, enabling users to input imaginary figures into models that may also contain real-world data. The potential outcomes of various courses of action can then be evaluated based upon figure projections. Our supermarket manager in the MIS example could perhaps view the potential impact on her profit margins of raising shelf prices, and all without having to enter into lengthy revenue calculations.

Decision support systems are most commonly used to aid strategic planning, as opposed to management information systems, which are more likely to guide operational decision making. Any DSS will therefore include access to external as well as internal company information. More importantly, a DSS will be far more flexible than a MIS, supporting rather than constraining the processing of data into information for management purposes.

## Executive information systems

**Executive information systems** are the most recent development in IS, although it is unclear as to whether they offer anything new, or simply provide the management information previously available via a MIS or a DSS in the form most useful to the decision taker (Martin and Powell, 1992: 187–8). The graphics and presentation facilities of an EIS will be far more advanced than in simple MIS or DSS systems, and the user interface is likely to be both friendly and highly interactive. Senior executives unwilling to become computer gurus or data analysis experts may therefore be enticed into using an EIS rather than other forms of information system.

Many executive information systems are simply an outgrowth of previous IS developments within the organization, perhaps augmented with new user interface technology. Being designed for top-level management purposes, executive information systems are arguably more likely to be used for problem finding rather than problem solving in comparison to earlier arrivals in the IS family. For example, the director of a supermarket chain may use an EIS to review turnover in each store and for each product brand on a weekly basis. Poor performances would thus be identified as problems, the solving of which would be delegated to individual store managers or corporate buyers.

*Office automation systems*

An **office automation system** (OAS) most frequently refers to a downsized, PC-based applications package used by either clerical or administrative personnel to ease the burden of office activity. Word processing packages, spreadsheets and databases, as detailed in chapter 2, are therefore the most common examples of an OAS. Electronic mail is another frequent OAS application that aims to make office activity more efficient and cost effective. Most office automation systems could be classed as simply downsized examples of DP, management information or decision support systems.

## Excellence and information systems

So far in this chapter we have discussed how IS can both automate and augment organizational and management activity by employing information technology. In doing so computer systems improve transaction processing and empower managers with performance feedbacks and information projections in order to aid decision making and improve task coordination. The potential for all forms of IS to improve corporate performance is therefore not in question, with the comparative advantage of many competing organizations now dependent on the quality of their information systems. Indeed as Davidow and Malone note as they look forward to the twenty-first century: 'In the years to come, incremental differences in companies' abilities to acquire, distribute, store, analyze, and invoke actions based upon information will determine the winners and the losers in the battle for customers' (Davidow and Malone, 1992: 50).

But how do successful organizations approach their information systems? In 1990 Management Science America (MSA) Ltd commissioned a qualitative survey to address this question, aiming to reveal the policies and attitudes towards IT implementation in successful British organizations. In-depth interviews with the top IT management of companies like ASDA, ICI and Grand Metropolitan were conducted, in addition to the collection of factual questionnaires. All the companies surveyed were deemed to be 'excellent' in terms of their profits, growth, reputation and market sector position. Some of the survey's key findings were as follows (MSA, 1990: 42):

- In excellent companies, IT strategy was inextricably linked to business strategy.
- Excellent companies did not use technology for technology's sake: they were 'early followers' and not pioneers.
- Training was crucially important for the successful operation of the IT department and also to retain scarce staff.
- IBM systems were the natural choice for most companies.
- Networking and distributed processing (downsizing) were of a major and increasing importance.
- Future IS planning was dependent on business planning and high-level management involvement.
- Two to three years were maximum realistic IS planning horizons.
- The ability to cope with growth necessitated flexibility in both the hardware and software employed in company systems.
- In two-thirds of the companies surveyed, most or some senior managers had PCs on their desks.

The overriding theme of the MSA survey was the increasing strategic importance of information technology application, and hence the IS link to overall business strategy. It is also interesting that the companies surveyed allowed others to be the trailblazers with new technologies and applications. They did not themselves want to be guinea-pigs, instead allowing their competitors to make mistakes and encounter system pitfalls. The significance of training, especially to retain quality IT personnel, and the requirement of IT flexibility to facilitate growth, were perhaps not that surprising. Finally the notion that the maximum realistic planning horizon was not be greater than three years should be remembered. Investing for the long-term future (within, for example, a ten-year strategic plan) is not generally an option in IS, due to the rampant pace of technological development.

## Strategy, information technology and information systems

Strategy is concerned with both planning and creating management systems that allow organizations to respond to an unknowable and unpredictable environment (Dobson and Starkey, 1993). Strategy concerning computer technology application may be approached from two angles. On the one hand, *IS strategy* is concerned with ascertaining an organization's demand for applications, whereas on the other, *IT strategy* will concern itself with how those demands are actually satisfied. The former, not surprisingly given the nature of IS, will be driven largely via in-depth business systems analysis. Strategy in IT, however, will be biased towards investigation and specification of the computer systems and applications to be employed to solve IS problems across the business. The distinction between strategy in information *technology* versus strategy in information *systems* can easily become blurred, with many organizations using the terms 'IS strategy' and 'IT strategy' interchangeably. Unfortunately, this can lead to the direction of the causality relationship between IS and IT being largely ignored.

### Business strategy and the IS/IT relationship

Ideally, strategy and resulting policy in IS will determine strategy and policy for IT. In other words, organizational requirements will determine the means sought to fulfil their technological solution. In many organizations this has not been the case. Instead, technological developments have driven IS thinking. One reason for this has been that many managers have long viewed IS strategy as only being concerned with computer technology, rather than the overall development of organization systems and hence processes. Business and IS strategy have therefore often been formulated in isolation, allowing expert power within the IT department to guide policy on IS. Hence it can be noted that the: 'Traditional IS mentality has generally focused on technology, not strategic business planning' (Larson and Zimney, 1990: 103). Or as Wyles notes: 'For too long, the gulf between IT managers and business managers has been allowed to widen until, in some organizations the tail is wagging the dog . .

. [and hence] . . . The IT department decides what is best for the business in terms of new equipment and new systems' (Wyles, 1992: 495).

To overcome this situation, both managers and their IS/IT departments and functions need to be made aware that IT implementation is about more than improving the efficiency of organization systems. It is also about increasing their overall *effectiveness*.

> Efficiency is about doing things right, but effectiveness is doing the right things. Doing the wrong things in a very efficient manner just means you waste less money! The correct use of IT can dramatically increase the company's ability to gain and sustain competitive edge, and that is the major battle above all others.   (Wyles, 1990: 495)

Successful IS strategic planning will therefore only result if senior management:

> communicate a clear vision of where the business is going and what challenges lie ahead, so appropriate productivity tools can be selected. Business strategy must drive IS strategy, but this can only happen if IS is part of the strategic planning process. . . .
>
> IS directors must be given the opportunity to expand their horizons, to understand the visionary perspectives of the CEO. They need to better appreciate the competitive challenges for the next ten years – as strategic thinkers and partners, not as technology hoarders.   (Larson and Zimney, 1990: 103)

With reference back to the MSA survey, the above can now be witnessed in successful organizations. Within these companies IT strategy is 'inextricably linked' to the strategy of the business as a whole, with future IT planning dependent on both business planning and high-level management involvement.

## Rallying support

Attempting to link IS strategy to overall corporate strategic planning can prove troublesome. IT systems and solutions have a tendency to become resource intensive, technically complex and shrouded in an incomprehensible jargon that alienates many potential advocates. Information systems may therefore fail to live up to expectations due to a lack of general support for their success across the organization that ultimately has to work with them.

Adriaans (1993: 45), for example, notes that although techniques for system implementation have been developed (as discussed in chapter 6), they are no guarantee of success because they tend to concentrate on the IS plan rather than the people involved. Therefore, IT strategies (supported at the highest level) should also be accompanied by an *information projects plan* (supported by grass-roots operational personnel), detailing the projects required to bridge the gap between the present and desired situation.

## *IT and competitive advantage*

There is a plethora of strategic literature pertaining to acquiring or increasing competitive advantage via IT implementation. Porter (1985) provides the basis for most analysis. He suggests that firms need to acquire a 'thorough understanding' of all the technologies in their 'value chain' in order to determine which may be improved to reap gains or enforcements in competitive advantage. Senker and Senker (1992) similarly note that a lack of knowledge and experience are a problem, that time is needed to understand new technologies, and that large investments in staff training are essential. The importance of possessing technical understanding in order to maximize system benefit implies that companies with cumulative expertise in new technologies will be in a stronger position to exploit IS/IT applications than many traditional organizations. Electronics manufacturers, for example, will be better placed to capitalize from computer-aided design compared to companies engaged in mechanical and electrical engineering (Senker and Senker, 1992: 31).

Success in gaining competitive advantage from IT systems is also dependent on attitude changes across the organization. Management must realize that changes in working practices will be required to capitalize on the benefits of IT. And this implies changes in *their* working practices as well as those of their subordinates. Managers in many firms are still not prepared to use PCs, instead banishing the hardware to their secretaries' desks and delegating a broad spectrum of applications from spreadsheet, database and accounting work to electronic mail communications (Senker and Senker, 1992: 38). This 'chauffeured' approach to PC implementation can perhaps be explained by a lack of basic PC management training, and is notable by its relative absence in organizations with a history of success in applying computer technology. The adoption of a PC by a manager, as well as improving their personal effectiveness, will also serve as an icon for change and new practice across the rest of the organization.

In addition to the acquisition of technological knowledge and changes in attitudes and hence working practices, levels of centralization are frequently cited as a determinant of success in organizational computer application. To a large degree the near-universal centralization of IT resources in previous years was due to the nature of mainframe technology, with decentralized processing options simply not being available. With the rise of the PC and downsized applications over the past decade, organizations now have a choice as to the level of implementation and control of their information systems. In particular *on-line transaction processing* (OLTP), essential in applications such as banking for real-time, interactive client feedback, may now be implemented on non-mainframe systems. Many, unfortunately, will still not believe it – even when presented with examples like the Richmond Savings Credit Union, a bank-cum-building society ranking in the North American top ten, which carries out *all* of its computer processing over an OLTP PC network (Wheatley, 1993). Decentralization *really is* a credible alternative for virtually *all* centralized IT applications, meaning that centralized systems now at least require some level of strategic justification.

## Centralization versus decentralization

The advantages of downsizing computer operations may be numerous and varied. For a start, there are likely to be substantial cost savings reaped from the move away from mainframes and towards distributed processing systems based upon small computers. The organization will also enjoy increased IS flexibility. Both of these benefits result largely from the open architecture of the IBM PC, its wide applications base, and continuous supplier development in the software and hardware marketplace.

An organization, for example, is unlikely to become 'stuck' with a clutch of IBM PCs or compatibles, since the machines may be easily applied to a range of applications even when they are no longer state of the art. Thus IBM PCs with 286 and 386 CPUs initially purchased for complex database and spreadsheet work may find themselves gainfully employed for word processing and communications purposes when their initial users acquire more modern machines. A redundant mainframe computer, on the other hand will be just that – redundant, and with little or no scrap or second-hand value. The move to downsize also brings with it flexibility in the software employed by end users, which may be easily upgraded (especially if accessed from just one server over a LAN) as publishers release updates of their popular programs.

Downsized computer systems also provide organizations with more system flexibility when they are in a period of expansion. Both personal computer and networking hardware and software may be purchased and installed incrementally as an organization's size dictates. In other words, for each new worker employed, the company simply has to purchase one extra PC and associated software licenses. Centralized mainframe systems, on the other hand, offer far less flexibility when system capacity is reached and no more terminal connections are available. Thus either the entire system will need to be upgraded, or else a second mainframe will need to be purchased, even though demand for processing capacity may have only increased by a small fraction. It therefore becomes easy to appreciate why distributed processing across PC networks was of a 'major and increasing importance' in MSA's 'excellent' organizations. It is similarly no surprise that two-thirds of senior managers in these companies had PCs on their desks.

Critics of the downsizing trend argue that in the long term a centralized consolidation of the IS resource will prove more cost-effective, and that the demise of the centralized mainframe has been greatly exaggerated. They also state that centralization creates clear career paths for IS/IT personnel, and that moves towards decentralization are in contention with the integration of company-wide information systems across business functions (Simson, 1990: 158). To many, such criticisms seem to be more concerned with defending employee interests in IT departments rather the organization's strategic position. Either that, or they are simply voiced in ignorance of what is now possible with downsized technology. As Trimmer notes, the relationship between the IT department and the rest of the firm is often 'not a particularly happy one' (1993: 1), most people are still not aware of what is technologically feasible, and 'Those requiring the most education are generally the most specialist technicians, and a certain percentage of these may be very resistant to new technologies' (Trimmer, 1993: 6).

There are also two points concerning downsizing that make it an easy target for vitreolic attack. Firstly, it has a very high user profile, with machines spread around the organization. Therefore, if they don't work, critics can make sure *everybody* knows about it. Secondly, downsizing is not the traditional way of doing things (Trimmer, 1993: 74–5) and consequently inevitably open to question and critical scrutiny.

Although most of the criticisms voiced by those espousing IS/IT centralization may now be parried by addressing either attitudes or technological awareness, it is possible to go overboard with downsizing and inadvertently lose control of IS/IT strategy. If this happens, incompatible systems and data structures may proliferate across different departments or even adjacent offices, leading to headaches with training, data compatibility and some forms of computer communication. To avoid this, many major companies, whilst embracing networking and the downsizing trend, stipulate tight guidelines as to what personal computer hardware or software may or may not be purchased. For example firms may decree that all PCs must be acquired from just one supplier, and will adopt one word processor, spreadsheet and database as organization-wide applications package standards. This avoids data incompatibilities, and perhaps more significantly reduces the need for software retraining as personnel move between divisions.

It should be remembered when appraising downsizing's strategic merits or drawbacks that many large players within the computer industry are casualties of its success to date and may therefore have a significant vested interest in slowing the trend. IBM in particular is suffering, with many of its traditional customers turning to smaller and less expensive downsized systems from other suppliers. The downsizing trend thus accounts to a large degree for IBM's $5bn losses in 1992 – the largest in corporate history (Wheatley, 1993).

Whatever its merits, the costs incurred in establishing extensive, closed-architecture mainframe systems prevent many organizations pursuing the downsizing pathway. It is therefore paradoxical that some of the organizations most dependent on IT, and who may have been highly innovative in its initial adoption, have become trapped with old, centralized systems. The risk of first-mover advantage evolving into first-mover disadvantage in any area of technology adoption is invariably high, and one reason why many organizations are now deciding to outsource their IS requirements.

## The outsourcing decision

> It used to be that large companies boasted about their internal computer capability. Now they're boasting about cutting back and farming it out. (Mandell, 1991: 51)

The above quote summarizes the attitude of an increasing number of major corporations to whom the risk of being left holding a technologically obsolete baby is just far too high. Across a range of industries large businesses such as American Standard, Eastman Kodak, General Motors Metropolitan Life and the Ford Motor Company are turning management of their big computers or data communications over to market specialists

(Mandell, 1991; Martinsons, 1993). Outsourcing IT operations can significantly reduce corporate vulnerability to risk – and for companies intent on using large computer systems, the risks of opting for the wrong system, or perhaps of being unable to downsize if needs arise, can be very high indeed.

Technological risk-aversion is not the only factor to be considered when contemplating the trade-out of IS and IT responsibility. For a start, the outsourcing decision may be taken simply to disband or curtail the powerbase of an IT department full of systems experts who will just not think like marketeers. Thus some firms may farm out their IT functions as an alternative to attempting to change the attitudes and skills of their internal staff. Similarly, outsourcing puts the control of IT exploitation back in the hands of managers to whom new subcontracted market agents will report. Contracted companies are far less likely to run around 'looking for problems to solve', and 'rarely solved on schedule'. Many executives are now cautious regarding the 'computer-as-a-saviour attitude', especially when they look across the ocean to the Japanese who are less reliant on computer systems and yet more successful in business (Mandell, 1991).

Farming out IT functions also frees organizations from the continuous and ardent battle to recruit and retain high-quality IT personnel. Many companies are now finding that they simply cannot hire enough high-calibre IT employees to maintain existing programs, let alone cope with new system requirements. The fact that professionals capable of managing large corporate networks are now paid up into 'the low six figures' only serves to indicate the severity of their supply shortage (Mandell, 1991: 51).

## Enter the systems integrators

Even companies who have decided not to trade out the running of their computer operations are now turning to the marketplace for the development and installation of their new computer solutions. Indeed, large downsized systems, although utilizing off-the-shelf hardware and software, may prove troublesome to introduce: 'Despite so-called open systems and huge efforts at computer standardisation, getting pieces of equipment from different manufacturers to work together can still be a nightmare' (Bird, 1993a: 83).

Companies may therefore turn to *systems integrators* in the open market to minimize system initiation risks. These firms specialize in translating business problems and specifications into IT solutions at guaranteed prices.

Systems integration contracts frequently improve cashflow, as companies will not be billed until their system is installed *and working*.

Systems integration is now one of the computer industry's biggest growth sectors, booming partly due to the increasing technical complexity of high-speed computer interconnection over telecom networks. This said, the systems integration sub-niche will probably enjoy short-lived success, as industry standards converge and systems become more tolerant of each other's little quibbles. It should be remembered that interactive, computer-network-centred business operations are a comparatively recent development, and still need professional nursemaids to aid them though difficult periods. We can, however, be fairly sure that:

> Piecing together the components of a technically complex system may one day become so easy that users can wheel their own trolley around the supermarket. Until then, the specialist catering companies of the IT world will still be called in for really important occasions.   (Bird, 1993a: 83)

### Summary

There is already a large family of information systems that may be employed to ease data handling and assist in managerial activity across most organizations. As new and radically different technology forms and applications emerge, there is an ever-present risk for organizations to become left behind if they do not keep up to date. At the other extreme, organizations also need to be careful that they do not inadvertently allow technology rather than business policy to guide their IS strategy. Attitudes to IS and IT across the organization will be as significant as technological competence in reaping competitive advantage from computer application in the future. This will apply especially with regard to the downsizing trend away from centralized mainframe systems and the possible decision to outsource IT responsibilities and operations.

This chapter has involved a wide-ranging coverage of management and information systems. A broad range of viewpoints from a variety of sources have been presented, which will hopefully allow interested readers to delve further into the discipline of IS and IT strategy. In particular chapter 5 has addressed:

- The nature of management, information and systems.
- The role of computers in improving cost-effectiveness, increasing business growth and aiding the decision process.

- The classification of data processing, management information, decision support, executive information and office automation systems (DPS, MIS, DSS, EIS and OAS).
- IT in 'excellent' organizations.
- Strategy, information systems and information technology
- Competitive advantage, the downsizing trend towards IT/IS decentralization, and the outsourcing decision.

## Review and discussion questions

1.  How may information systems improve both management control and strategic decision making?
2.  Explain some of the common pitfalls into which companies may descend when formulating IT strategy.

# 6 Implementing computer solutions

Computers cause problems for both people and organizations. In particular, any moves to introduce or upgrade computer-based work systems will bring with them a diverse spectrum of hurdles. Firstly, the tasks any system is to perform will need to be carefully specified and a methodology for their accomplishment determined. A changeover strategy between the old and the new must also be formulated, as must alterations to working practices to enable efficient operation of the new system. There may also be employee concerns regarding occupational health hazards to allay and workplace ergonomics legislation to be adhered to. Finally, even if all these fences are cleared without penalty, organizations may still experience both management and worker resistance to new computer systems. Employee skills and attitudes may therefore be potential key determinants of any new system's success or failure.

Unfortunately, it is all too easy to dismiss the theory and gallop foolhardily ahead when computer solutions are being sought. Especially when budgets or deadlines are tight and managers fear for their skins if schedules from whip-crackers on-high are not strictly adhered to. Most organizations, however, have a horror story or two to tell regarding instances when system development went disastrously wrong. The abandonment of the UK stock market's *Taurus* system at an estimated cost of over £400m is perhaps one of the most public of tales. There are also an increasing number of claims arising against organizations brought by employees whose health has apparently been impaired by workplace computer usage. Patience and detailed investigation should therefore clearly be noted as virtuous when computer systems are being initiated or upgraded. Grass-roots planning leaving most stones displaced *has* to be undertaken. Similarly, worker concerns must not be bulldozed. The old adage 'more haste, less speed' also springs to mind as essential mental fodder for managers caught up in the steeplechase of system development.

## Managing systems development

Broadly defined, systems development involves analysing information needs, deciding on hardware requirements, agreeing specifications with user departments, software development and testing, and finally the process of implementation (Martin and Powell, 1992: 193). The discipline is therefore both a complex and challenging occupation, requiring the integration of people from many different specialisms, usually brought together in project teams. Because systems development is about much more than simply hardware acquisition and writing or buying-in software, failures tend to be commonplace. As already noted with the *Taurus* example, system failures can lead to financial disaster. They may also endanger lives – as happened when the London Ambulance Service's system failed in 1992. These two instances are, of course, extreme cases, although few new systems are a roaring success:

> Some manage to operate, at least in part, just below the standards set by their original design specifications, while others respond well to heavy demand on certain functions but very poorly when it comes to others. There are many diverse reasons for the shortfall in expected performance: poor design concepts, inability to determine in advance the range and depth of users' needs, rigidity that prevents easy modifications capable of keeping up with circumstances, and so on.   (Eilon, 1993: 135)

Bearing these points in mind, and also the fact that any new system will inevitably redefine the task structure, and hence the social fabric, of the parts of the organization it impacts upon, three key issues in systems development should be of particular managerial concern:

- the importance of planning;
- the impact on people; and
- the role of communications.

### *The importance of planning*

The introduction of a new computer-based work system will require far more upfront forethought than necessary in the establishment of a new set of human-centred working practices. The criticality of computer system preplanning stems from the fact that information technology tends to have a far lower flexibility tolerance than that possessed by most employees.

Human beings exhibit tremendous adaptive abilities when thrown into new situations, and will rapidly climb a learning curve to storm towards efficient operations. Computer systems, on the other hand, are far less adaptive and will simply perform exactly as programmed, and with largely constant efficiency, from day one. It therefore becomes paramount to get a computer system as near perfect as possible from the start. For although its human operators may be left to evolve rapidly and fine-tune themselves into new working practices, the computer system itself will require expensive reprogramming if task sequences and operational requirements need to be altered. You cannot just muddle through for the first month or two with a new computer system and hope it will work itself out. It won't, as users will invariably have little or no control over its adaptation.

## The impact on people

The scale of the changes required in workplace practices resulting from the introduction of computer systems are at times staggering. Consider the impact on the draughtsman, for example, once seated with pen or pencil at slanted board and the centre of design, specification and drafting activity. Now working with a computer-aided design (CAD) system:

> . . . the draughtsman no longer needs to produce a drawing and so the subtle interplay of interpretation and modification as the commodity was being designed and related to skilled workers on the shop floor, is being ruptured. What the draughtsman now does is work on the digitiser and input material through a graticule or teletype. An exact reading is set of the length of each line, and the tolerance and other details. The design comes out as a tape which is expanded in the computer after which it operates some item of equipment such as a jig borer or a continuous path milling machine.   (Cooley, 1987: 60)

The above example serves to illustrate how many jobs may either be deskilled, or require new skills acquisition, after the introduction of information technology. Most significantly, for many workers their tacit understanding of the principles, knowledge and mathematics of their job will be abstracted away from the labour process when computers are introduced. Accountants familiar with double-entry in paper volumes may therefore resist ledgers that exist only as bit patterns within computer chips and as magnetic recordings on floppy disks.

The shift towards computerization at work may also shift the focus of office activity away from people and towards technology. In previous years accounts clerks tended to be highly mobile within the office, with piles of paperwork moving between desks and being deposited within and extracted from rows of filing cabinets. The clerks themselves were the focus of work activity, and social interaction in the workplace was high. With computer-based accounting systems work activities now tend to be centred around VDU screens, decreasing the potential for social interplay. It is perfectly possible for many clerks to spend their entire day staring at a screen and typing at a keyboard.

The emergence of so-termed *office factories* could be seen to have led to deskilling and knowledge obsolescence for some, placed insurmountable new skills mountains before others, and reduced opportunities for workplace socialization. It is therefore no wonder that many people fear and hence resist moves to implement computer systems. So managers must move cautiously, aware that the benefits of the new system as viewed from on high may be perceived as drawbacks from a grass-roots point of view. Hence it is vital that new systems are explained to employees from the earliest opportunity and that adequate training in their operation is provided. Managers must also be prepared to adopt a supportive and sympathetic attitude during the nerve-wracking period of changeover between systems.

## The role of communications

One of the reasons for constructing detailed plans is to improve communications between the people involved in systems development. Many failures in systems implementation can be traced back to breakdowns in communication. Commonly, different developers may end up working to different timescales and specifications. Managing communications, particularly in the case of large projects, is therefore a crucial managerial task to ensure that both tasks and responsibilities are clearly specified and understood.

Feedbacks on performance to date, and between systems developers and end-users, also play an important role, allowing any required corrective actions to be undertaken as the earliest possible juncture. Formal systems review procedures are often implemented during long projects. Well-managed communications, if concentrating on stressing the long-term benefits of a new system throughout its development, will also serve to gain the commitment of all involved parties (Lambert, 1993).

## The systems development lifecycle

Most systems development analysis concentrates on a traditional 'lifecycle' model conceived back in the days of mainframe-only computing. Typically, systems analysts will devise the specifications for new systems, which will then be passed on to hardware specialists and applications programmers. Six phases are usually isolated across the development lifecycle, progressing as illustrated in figure 6.1.

Although of most significance in the development of new large-scale systems by analysts and project teams, the lifecycle model also provides a useful developmental checklist for the development of even simple, stand-alone PC applications. The analysis contained within its phases also

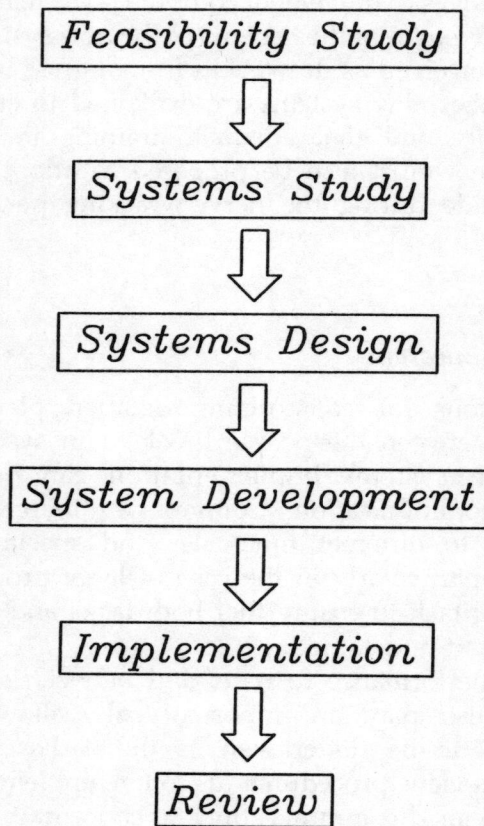

$$\boxed{Feasibility\ Study}$$

$$\Downarrow$$

$$\boxed{Systems\ Study}$$

$$\Downarrow$$

$$\boxed{Systems\ Design}$$

$$\Downarrow$$

$$\boxed{System\ Development}$$

$$\Downarrow$$

$$\boxed{Implementation}$$

$$\Downarrow$$

$$\boxed{Review}$$

**Figure 6.1**   The systems development lifecycle

contributes to other systems development methodologies. Thus, although the lifecycle development paradigm may appear long and cumbersome when first encountered, its stages and their sequential progression cannot be ignored.

## The feasibility study

The feasibility study is the first stage of any major project. Undertaken by senior personnel, it will question whether it is worthwhile proceeding in the development of a new system via appraising whether it would entail an efficient application of resources. The costs of proceeding versus not proceeding will therefore be balanced, a process usually entailing *cost–benefit analysis*.

### Feasibility cost–benefit analysis

Cost–benefit analysis attempts to put figures on all the potential costs and benefits of a new system, which will only become feasible if the latter measure exceeds the former. The new system scenarios with the greatest cost–benefit margin will be the ones chosen for further development. The success of cost-benefit analysis is dependent upon all feasible system alternatives being examined. This in turn implies that all costs and benefits associated with each new system scenario must be identified and measured in comparable (and usually financial) terms. In practice this is unlikely to be the case, and management will have to make subjective judgements in estimating the costs and benefits to the organization of any new system in both the short and long term.

The system costs to be considered in a feasibility analysis will be concerned with both system implementation and future operations. *Implementation costs* are likely to include:

- programming costs;
- hardware and software purchases;
- staff training/retraining costs;
- data conversion costs; and
- the productivity loss as a new learning curve is ascended.

*System running costs*, to be compared with the costs of operating any existing system, will result from expenses factors such as:

- data preparation (e.g. the batching and coding of invoices);

- computer consumables (e.g. floppy disks and printer forms); and
- software and hardware maintenance (including estimated system downtime losses).

The benefits resulting from potential new systems may be even more difficult to quantify in advance, though will usually centre around:

- reduced staff costs (in terms of both wages/salaries and overheads);
- improved sales, cashflow and/or profits;
- improved customer service;
- decreased stock-holding costs;
- improved management information and/or strategic planning; and
- improved employee relations/morale and corporate image.

### *The feasibility report*

Once the costs and benefits of any or all potential new systems have been evaluated, a feasibility report will be prepared. This document will comment upon the realism of attaining any new system requirements, the principle work areas concerned, the scope for attaining benefits, and any specialist assistance or expertise that may be necessary for implementation (Clifton, 1986: 184–5). After the presentation of the feasibility report, management will be in an informed position to make a decision on committing organizational resources to a new system. If a green light is given to proceed, a far more detailed, grass-roots investigation will then take place.

### The systems study

The systems study is the major investigatory stage, involving an analysis of the present system in order to ascertain new requirements and specifications. Engaging in a systems study enables the new system to capitalize on the merits of the old system, whilst hopefully minimizing its drawbacks. Many detailed questions will therefore need to be addressed in order to establish:

- the inputs to the present system;
- the objectives of the present system;
- the outputs of the present system;
- what information is currently produced;
- what additional information would prove valuable;

- what problems are currently experienced; and
- what additional functions could aid operation.

## Gathering data

In many cases, gathering data on the above can prove surprisingly difficult – many companies do not know *exactly* how their present systems actually work. As mentioned previously, this may not be a problem with a manual system, as people are adaptable and will cope with contingencies. Exacting operational specifications are, of course, required for computer systems. It is therefore amazing that many large organizations will leap headlong into the specification of a new computer system without gaining a detailed knowledge of how their old system works. In particular, user-perceived strengths and flexibilities should be accounted for. Cries of 'I used to be able to do that very easily, but now it takes forever' will do nothing to allay worker resistance to the new system or permit a smooth period of implementation.

Most systems studies make use of existing documentation, workplace observation, and end-user questionnaires and interviews, in obtaining information about the present system. Existing system documentation may include reference manuals and books of procedures (if available!), together with samples of all the paperwork, records and other output used in everyday operation. All this documentation, however, will tend to convey how the present system *should* work, rather than how it actually *does*. It can therefore not be relied upon as the sole data source.

Workplace observation will usually provide a totally different perspective on the present system than obtained via the inspection of documentation. It ought to be remembered, however, that findings will be potentially blinkered towards the observer's point of view, and that workers may behave differently when being watched. Such problems aside, workplace observation often exposes major operational difficulties and bottlenecks, as well as revealing key system strengths.

Questionnaires and interviews will be the most likely forum for collecting the crucial information encoded via experience into people's heads. Questionnaires will be essential when dealing with large numbers of current users, although they will need careful planning if they are not to lead respondents in certain directions. Interviews, on either an individual or group basis, can be more open-ended and will usually provide the best insights into current working practices. They will also allow suggestions to be voiced, and may even play a role in employee motivation by securing commitment to the project.

From its detailed analysis of the present system, coupled with an understanding of any new requirements, the systems study will provide a detailed specification of what any new system *should* do. It will not necessarily describe *how* the new system will achieve its operations – a task left to the following stage of *systems design*.

## Systems design

Following the systems study, *systems design* concerns the process of planning how the new system will work, and will detail the methods to be used in fulfilling its specification. Resulting from the systems design will be a specific *systems specification* in terms of data structures, working practices, and the software and hardware necessary to run the new system. Usually several technically feasible alternatives will present themselves during the design stage, and hence choices for the final specification will have to be made. Factors to be taken into account when making systems design choices include information requirements and user preferences, performance and reliability requirements, the implementation timescale, maintenance characteristics, and even management style and organizational culture (Martin and Powell, 1992: 205).

### End-user preferences and system ownership

Although the choice in deciding software and hardware requirements may be determined to a large degree by cost–benefit analysis, taking into account the comments and preferences of users may prove critical for long-term success. The 'classic' approach to systems design has been 'hit and run', with analysts appearing in the workplace, asking users strange questions, and some time after imposing a complete new system upon them. Such an approach alienates users, whereas incorporating their ideas can have the reverse effect and make them feel that any new system is 'really theirs'. Senker and Senker, for example, note that: 'Experience has shown that involving secretaries in the selection of equipment to be used for word processing yields considerable benefits, including better trained secretaries committed to the new technology and competent to produce professional standards of work' (1992: 38). Similarly, Alter (1980) addressed the *system ownership* factor in a system's success via an investigation of user involvement and user resistance in a study of fifty-six new decision support systems. Where final end-users had helped initiate the new system, there was significantly less resistance to their implementation. Additionally, of the fifteen new systems that experienced 'significant' user resistance, eleven had been developed with low user involvement.

## Technical specifications

Systems design also needs to consider certain technical specifications, for example:

- system type and hardware specification;
- input and output design;
- data structures and processing operations; and
- storage media and back-up procedures.

## System type and hardware specification

System type will be either *batch* or *realtime*. Batch systems exist where data is passed in bulk sequentially between processes. The payroll for each month, for example, being run as one batch. As another example, banks process all their customer statements and account balance changes overnight in one batch. At the other end of spectrum, realtime systems (also known as *interactive* or *on-line* systems), provide immediate responses to individual input requests and transactions. Immediate feedback is vital for systems that are employed for direct customer contact, such as those used to make travel reservations or process telephone sales.

Hardware specifications will only have to be recommended in situations where computing capacity does not already exist, or is inadequate to cope with new processing operations. The choice will be between a mainframe or minicomputer with linked terminals, a network of PCs based around a central server, or perhaps some combination.

## Input and output design

Input and output design will define how data is to be collected and how outputs from the system will be presented and distributed. Many factors will therefore be involved, from the layout of software data entry and display screens to the design of invoices and other forms of computer stationery. Input design may also include the specification of bar codings or other modes of item identification if data is to be captured automatically rather than via operator keying.

## Data structures and processing operations

Data structures and processing operations will need to be defined both for and by systems programmers who will create or customize the system software. As mentioned in chapter 2, when databases are being created, the structure of their files and records will need to be designed. The nature and length of their component fields will also need to be specified. Processing operations will govern how data is actually manipulated within the system – how accounts ledgers are reconciled, for example. Within many system routines, *check-sums* and other data validation measures will be included at key stages of processing to in order to minimize potential errors. For example, users may be required to enter invoices into the system in batches of ten or twenty. After the entry of each batch the computer will indicate a *batch total* of the cumulative value entered which must match with a precalculated, user-entered figure in order for processing operations to proceed.

## Storage media and back-up procedures

Finally, the media for the storage and back-up of information will need to be specified, and may include floppy disks, hard disks, optical disks and tape streamers (see chapter 3). Procedures for data back-up should also be defined so that users get into the habit of copying data to a secure location at frequent intervals.

## Flowcharts and the final specification

When user requirements have been considered and technical criteria finalized, a specific, highly detailed specification for the new system will result. This will frequently include **flowcharts** illustrating data processing and the progression of workflows throughout the system. The sight of such a drawing in a system analyst's clutches is enough to intimidate many otherwise robust managers into subservience. It should therefore be remembered that flowcharts are produced as graphical *aids* in order to *simplify* the communication of information pertaining to a system, and may even prove useful! This does not imply, of course, that all those who may at some point in time become entangled in systems development should become flowcharting experts. It is wise, however, to know the common symbols so that charts thrust in your direction do not appear as Greek as the pillars of an Athenian temple. Figure 6.2 serves as an illustration of the common flowcharting symbols and their interconnection. In particular note that a rectangle is used to represent processing, a trapezium for input or output, and a diamond when decisions are to occur.

## System development

System development involves the translation of a detailed new system specification into final, operation-ready software running on the appropriate hardware. In general, most system development time and

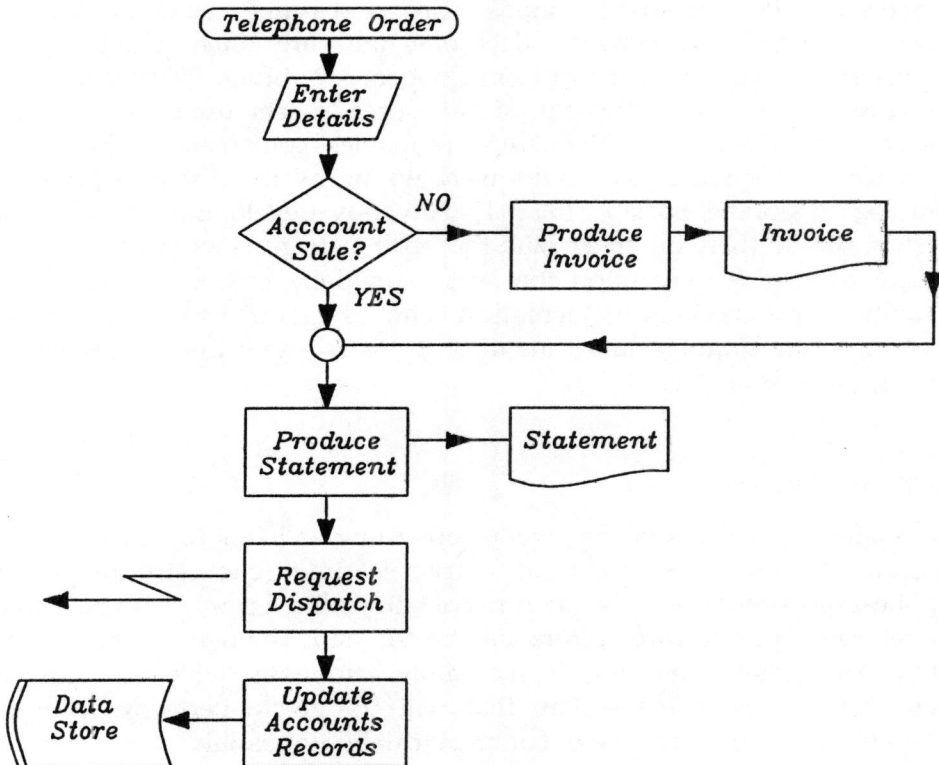

**Figure 6.2**   Example of a flowchart

money is expended on program coding and compilation. Staggeringly, American businesses have spent over $2 trillion on programming since the computer was invented (Rochester and Rochester, 1991: 247). Large projects involving computer networks and communications may also entail time-consuming and expensive hardware installation – e.g. proving ethernet cabling to every user-point in a large building or office complex.

## Testing! Testing!

Testing forms a vital component of the system development phase. Most systems programs and many hardware installations will fail to operate successfully at the first attempt, and even minor errors can cause major headaches when systems go live. Indeed, when developing large systems, more time will be spent in testing and quality control than in actual specification and programming.

Testing is not only important when large systems are being developed. Stand-alone PC spreadsheet models are increasingly used to support major financial and strategic decisions, and are often produced by managers themselves. A report from Coopers & Lybrand Deloitte in 1992, however, noted that nine out of ten spreadsheets used for decision analysis in a range of blue chip companies contained at least one significant error such that results were wrong by more than 5 per cent (Strategic Planning Society, 1992: 1). Anybody developing any scale of system should therefore make sure that each element is working correctly before coming to rely upon the system in daily business usage. This usually means checking mathematical routines against hand calculations, and executing dummy data runs in order to ascertain that processing is taking place as it should.

## Error strategies

No system, regardless of the level of pretesting, is likely to be developed without errors. Even common market-leading, competition-slaying applications programs are known to contain coding errors or **bugs**. Three distinct strategies towards errors may be adopted. The first is simply *error prevention*, where checking is incredibly strenuous with the aim of delivering an error-free system that will co-operate perfectly with its users from day one. This is, of course, virtually impossible.

Two more realistic error strategies concern themselves with error *detection* or error *tolerance*. Error detection focuses attention on making sure that errors are highlighted for correction once operations have begun. Error tolerance is the policy of designing systems so that if failures do occur they will not prove catastrophic. This *fail-soft* approach may permit operations to continue even after errors have occurred, perhaps by allowing the isolation of failed components coupled with automatic switching to alternatives. Most large systems will be developed with rapid error detection and high error tolerance in mind. Most organizations can cope with errors – providing they know that they have occurred.

## System implementation

Once the hurdles of feasibility, specification, design and implementation have been cleared, a new system enters the nail-biting phase of *implementation*. It is at this point that all the grand ideas actually come into play, with the new system becoming the system on which managers and end-users will be dependent during organizational life.

Leaving aside for the moment concerns regarding employee attitudes and new social patterns, system implementation basically involves four elements:

- preparation of the workplace;
- data conversion;
- staff training; and
- selecting a changeover strategy.

### *Preparation of the workplace*

Preparing the workplace for the operation of a new system may mean simply the replacement of certain items of hardware. On a grander scale, workplace preparation may require the entire redesign of seating and other arrangements to accommodate new computers, printers, wiring and communications hardware. Tighter security arrangements may have to be brought into play if a once technology-free office is suddenly to be occupied by tens of thousands of pounds worth of computing equipment. Measures to ensure power supplies are never cut off or interrupted may also prove necessary. Finally, lighting installations may have to be altered to avoid reflections on VDU screens, and even air-conditioning may have to be adjusted to provide a suitable working environment for delicate electronic equipment. Most of these measures come under the heading of *office ergonomics*, and are discussed in a wider context later in this chapter.

## Data conversion

Converting data from one system to another can be a real headache – even if the conversion is simply between an old and a new computer system. Customer and supplier details, ledger codes, stock lists and personnel records – all these and more will need to be converted into file structures compatible with the new system. Invariably, despite advances in computer technology, conversion is undertaken by obtaining printouts from the old system and manually rekeying the information into the new one. Surprisingly, this operation is often allocated to temporary staff who cannot reasonably be expected to foster any real commitment to the new system or the accuracy of the data held within it. If this method of data conversion is utilized, the rekeyed data must be at the very least be checked by one senior member of staff. A system can be no better than the working data on which it is based. It thus remains a mystery why many companies flinch at the prospect of additional expense or time delay at the data conversion stage and rush through the process as quickly and cheaply as possible.

As computer technology develops, it is likely that problems in data conversion between systems will be considerably eased, with translations between different hardware and software formats becoming commonplace. Even when data is converted electronically, it is still worth checking its integrity as so much depends on the accuracy of the core information within any system.

## Staff training

As noted at the start of this chapter, any system is only as good as the people who operate it. Training in new working practices is vital for new system success, although often systems analysts do not give training the attention it deserves, instead being more concerned with the computer hardware and software (Capron and Perron, 1993: 280). A good time to start user training is during the system development testing phase, so that employees can gain off-job experience of the new system in a comparatively stress-free environment. The provision of adequate training manuals can also be vital – especially if a new, downsized system uses off-the-shelf software with which users may wish to experiment. Even with significant resources devoted to training and learning resources, a short-term productivity decrease in the period after implementation has to be expected when any new system comes into operation.

## Selecting a changeover strategy

The strategy employed in the changeover between an old and a new system will be determined largely by the risk of failures versus the costs involved. In general, the safer the strategy adopted, the more it will cost. Although many hybrid forms may be identified in practice, there are four main strategies for new system implementation:

- direct cut-over;
- parallel running;
- pilot running; and
- phased conversion.

## Direct cut-over

Direct cut-over implies a direct switch between two systems: one day you use the old system, the next day you employ the new one. This is clearly the lowest-cost changeover scenario, but highly risky. If something goes wrong, you have no fall-back and must fix it. For most organizations, such a risk needs to be carefully weighed.

## Parallel running

In contrast to direct cut-over, parallel running offers the safest means of switching between systems. Here the old and the new are run side by side for a certain time – perhaps for a week or a month – to alleviate the risks should the new system fail. Usually the new system is used as the 'real' one, and the old run as a back-up. Parallel running allows new system outputs to be checked against the old system, and can therefore aid in error detection. The main problems associated with this approach stem from the expense involved in running two systems together, and potential logistical difficulties. Will the office accommodate two systems at once, for example? And will double the number of staff be needed? And if extra staff are employed, will they run the old system or the new?

A final problem may arise when the end of the parallel running period is on the horizon. Employees frequently request the continuation of two systems in tandem, having become reliant on *both*. Managers therefore have to be resolute in enforcing the period of system duplication. Although expensive, a parallel running changeover strategy is commonly employed where critical systems are concerned, such as those in banks and other financial institutions on which so many business operations now rely.

## Pilot running

With pilot running a new system is directly introduced (without parallel back-up) in just one area or division of the organization. Only part of the organization is thus subjected to potential new system risks, yet live running occurs. Changes can therefore be enacted before the entire organization engages in changeover to the new system. Pilot running is therefore cheaper than parallel running, though with less risk involved than with a direct cut-over policy. The strategy is particularly useful when advanced technology is being introduced into an organization for the first time, or when the organization concerned is inexperienced in management of the change process.

## Phased conversion

Finally there is the strategy of phased conversion. This again lies between direct cut-over and parallel running in terms of cost and risk exposure. Rather than requiring total implementation in one department or division, phased conversion infers that new, large systems will go live one stage at a time. For example, everybody will begin using the new stock control system, but not the new accounting or payroll system. A period between the initiation of each segment of the system is allowed to check all is working satisfactorily before the next stage is implemented. As with pilot running, only part of the organization bears risks at any one point in time.

Phased conversion can, of course, only occur when the particular modules of a new system can be isolated and run independently. With increased links and communications between users across different organizational functions, the possibilities for applying a phased conversion system implementation strategy may diminish in the future.

## System review

Almost as soon as a new system is up and running, changes will be needed, maintenance will be required, and expansions may be initiated. Indeed, with rapid organizational growth, continual developments in information technology, and turbulent product markets, some companies will find themselves faced with near-constant systems development. Even if this is not the case, reviewing the development lifecycle after its completion may signal useful lessons to be applied in future systems projects. The development of any system will inevitably have consumed a large quantity of staff time and other organizational resources. It is therefore only prudent to extract as much information as possible from a review of the progress of the project – especially if the system created has not lived up to expectations.

## Other approaches to system development

The six-stage lifecycle model is generally applied in the development and implementation of large, custom-created systems. Other routes for system development and implementation come classed under the headings of:

- prototyping;
- the critical success factors approach; and
- packaged software and end-user computing.

### *Prototyping development*

Whereas the systems development lifecycle focuses on tight project management to ensure system requirements are achieved, the prototyping methodology concentrates on building a working model so that users can identify their requirements. Prototypes will therefore simulate the functionality, operations or representations of potential systems, and should be cheap to develop (Preece, 1993: 104). Prototyping is employed where the precise requirements for a new system may be difficult to identify – e.g. when employees have no previous knowledge of computer operations. The creation of a model helps users to understand how a computer system may assist them in their work, and serves as a starting point for the definition of the final system. Sometimes many different features are built into a prototype so that users can choose the modes of operation they find most comfortable. For example, several different variants of data entry screen may be prototyped from which users will pick the best to be implemented in the final system.

Prototype systems may be developed in two forms: *throwaway* and *evolutionary* (Alter, 1992: 663). Throwaway prototypes are systems designed purely to test ideas and operational functions. They will therefore be scrapped once a final specification has been agreed and a new system constructed from scratch. Evolutionary prototypes, on the other hand, will be continually adapted as their specifications become firmly cast and will evolve into the final working system.

## The critical success factors approach

The critical success factors (CSF) approach focuses on identifying the key performance indicators or factors most critical in an organization's success. Examples of such factors may include the return on investment (ROI) and market share figures. Any information system will therefore be designed to support the achievement of these factors and hence the performance of the organization as a whole. The method encourages managers to isolate the factors most important to them in running the business, and hence the forms of information system that may be most gainfully developed. A CSF approach is likely to be implemented during resource allocation when organizations are having to decide where new computer systems would prove most effective. The approach is also used in the design of executive information systems. Here managers will probably be able to isolate the critical factors that guide their decisions, but may be unable to become embroiled in a lengthy analysis of information flows (Martin and Powell, 1992: 233).

## Applications packages and end-user computing

In organizations where the downsizing trend is in full swing and PCs have proliferated, many new computer systems will be developed by end-users tailoring standard applications packages to their own requirements. Most commonly, such systems will be based upon spreadsheets, databases or PC accounts packages. The advantages of systems driven by the needs of end-users, and based on applications packages are numerous. Most notably such systems are cheap, their development is focused exclusively on task requirements, commitment to success is high, and the end-user's knowledge of the final system will be considerable. Disadvantages may stem from the fact that end-users may not approach system development in a structured fashion, and may not have the expertise to create optimal and rigorously tested solutions. End-user system development should certainly not be discouraged, however, as it fosters commitment and work-centred learning in business computing development.

## Office ergonomics and occupational health

Ergonomics is concerned with the study of people in relationship to their environment, and the design and manipulation of that environment for comfort, safety and efficiency (Preece, 1992: 127). The discipline is therefore closely related to that of occupational health, which considers the whole spectrum of physical and mental well-being at work. Both fields of study are of increasing concern with regard to both the implementation of computer systems, and in particular the long-term impacts of working with information technology.

Well-designed and ergonomically optimal environments allow people to work both efficiently and in comfort. At the polar extreme of the scale, poor workplace ergonomics lead to occupational health complaints and associated legal actions for damages against employers. The latter issue is increasingly prominent since the introduction in 1993 of the European Community Health and Safety Directive 90/270/EEC concerning minimum health and safety requirements for employees who 'habitually work with display screen equipment'.

## Physical health complaints

Physical health complaints resulting from constant computer usage are now widespread. Walk around any large, computer-populated office and you will hear moans and groans pertaining to eyestrain, headaches and pains in body parts as diverse as fingers, wrists, shoulders, backs and thighs. However much toil computers may liberate office workers from, there is definitely a price to be paid in terms of physical comfort. Most health complaints encountered can be classed within the following three categories:

- eye complaints and headaches;

- aches and pains; and
- repetitive strain injuries.

### Eye complaints and headaches

Most people who use a VDU suffer from associated eye problems from time to time. Complaints range from sore eyes, eyestrain, burning sensations and eye tics, to conjunctivitis, cataracts, blurred vision and fatigue. And if you already have difficulties with your eyes or wear contact lenses, any problems are likely to be aggravated by using a VDU (Wood, 1992: 105). Only the increased risk of cataracts catalysed by VDU emissions has yet to be proven conclusively. About other complaints there is now no reasonable debate. Computer screens demand that workers stare continuously at fixed-distance images, in turn tensing their eye muscles and reducing their rate of natural blinking. Eye dryness may also result from air conditioning systems in modern buildings, which are frequently designed with the comfort of computers rather than human workers in mind.

The true impact of computer usage on people's eyesight is yet to be discovered. Only decades hence, when we have a retiring generation who have worked all their lives at VDU screens, will the true extent of the problem be revealed. By then, of course, it will be too late for many and irreparable damage will have been done. Potential 'solutions' and EC recommendations on screen ergonomics follow later in this section. One possible way to reduce eye strain that can be easily adopted by any user, however, is to close your eyes for 10–15 seconds every so often (Ross et al., 1992: 163).

Frequent computer users also complain of headaches, which are often associated with (if not indistinguishable from) eye problems. Headaches may also result from a build up of static electricity around high-voltage equipment like monitors and laser printers. The drone and clatter of an impact printer may also aggravate a headache, as may the background whine of noisy computer cooling fans from which many employees cannot escape throughout their entire working day.

### Aches and pains

Lower back pain is common amongst computer users due to the static posture induced when working at a screen and keyboard combination. Neck, leg and shoulder pains may also result from long sessions before a

VDU. It is therefore recommended that computer users adopt a range of postures during the working day to alleviate aches and pains – particularly back pains, which can develop into musculo-skeletal disorders. Excessive fatigue can also result from posture problems, with aches and pains leading some people to feel overtired or even depressed.

## Repetitive strain injuries

Repetitive strain injury (RSI), also termed *upper limb disorder* or *cumulative trauma disorder* is related to various conditions affecting fingers, wrists, forearms and shoulders. The condition results from excessive repetitive dexterous operations, such as continuous high-speed typing. Many employees can average between 15,000 and 20,000 keystrokes per hour at a computer keyboard, and some are touching 27,000. A 'safe limit' is perhaps a maximum of 10,000 keystrokes on an hourly basis (Wood, 1992).

Early signs of RSI include a tingling or numbness in the fingers, and pain or even swelling across the hands or upper arms. These symptoms may indicate either tenosynovitis (swollen muscles), or carpal tunnel syndrome (swollen tendons). RSI is now a widespread and serious occupational condition of which all employers must be aware. In the United States, the National Institute of Occupational Health and Safety has reported that 40 per cent of employees working predominantly with VDUs suffer RSI symptoms, with 12–15 per cent experiencing constant discomfort (Ross et al., 1992: 164). In the UK, at one point in time 130 journalists on the *Financial Times* were reported to be suffering from RSI, with at least twelve on long-term sick leave (Eade, 1992: 299). It is therefore no surprise that claims for RSI occupational injury compensation are now coming to court. In the United Kingdon one of the first test cases involved twelve workers from British Telecom, where staff were paid on a keystrokes-per-hour basis (Wood, 1992).

## Radiation concerns

In addition to the above complaints, some users and analysts are expressing as yet unproven concerns regarding the dangers of long-term exposure to VDU radiation emissions. In some cases it has been suggested that the **very low frequency (VLF) ionizing radiation** emitted by CRT monitor screens has been the cause of skin sores and rashes. Studies by some scientists have also suggested that there is an increased risk of cancer resulting from overexposure to VDU radiation, and that foetuses may be endangered. Others dismiss these claims as scaremongering, pointing out that the electromagnetic emissions people receive at work from computer screens are far lower than the doses they soak-up from the sun or domestic appliances like television sets. At present there is no clear picture on this issue, with some people believing: 'that studies illustrating a possible link between radiation and cancer, birth defects or miscarriages cannot be ignored, [whilst] others say only a crank could think sitting in front of a monitor could be dangerous' (Eade, 1992: 300).

## Containing health risks: the ideal workplace

With the wide range of potential computer-related health problems in mind, many attempts are now being made to minimize the risks involved in working with information technology. Some measures incur virtually no costs (e.g. rearranging VDUs so that they do not face the window), whilst others (involving major office equipment replacement) can cost a lot of money. What follows is a brief summary of measures intended to improve workplace ergonomics which incorporate the minimum requirements for display equipment as defined by the EC Health and Safety Directive (HSD).

## Optimal VDU ergonomics

Problems associated with VDU equipment are probably of greatest concern to both computer users and on-the-ball company lawyers. Figure 6.3 illustrates a common amalgamation of best practice in the provision and layout of computer equipment. In particular the following should be noted.

### *Monitor height, position and filter*

The monitor provided should be separate from the keyboard with its swivel and tilt freely adjustable by the user. The top of the screen should be at about eye level, meaning that the user's head will be comfortably angled when viewing the screen. A filter may be fitted to the monitor, hinged to a fixing atop the unit to allow regular cleaning. Screen filters are available in a variety of guises – the best (and most expensive) models reduce glare, increase display contrast, ground all static emission, and cut electro-

Eyes level with
top of screen

Screen Filter

Angled VDU

Ample
leg
room

Desk
Height
70cm

Chair with
adjustable
back & height

Angled Footrest

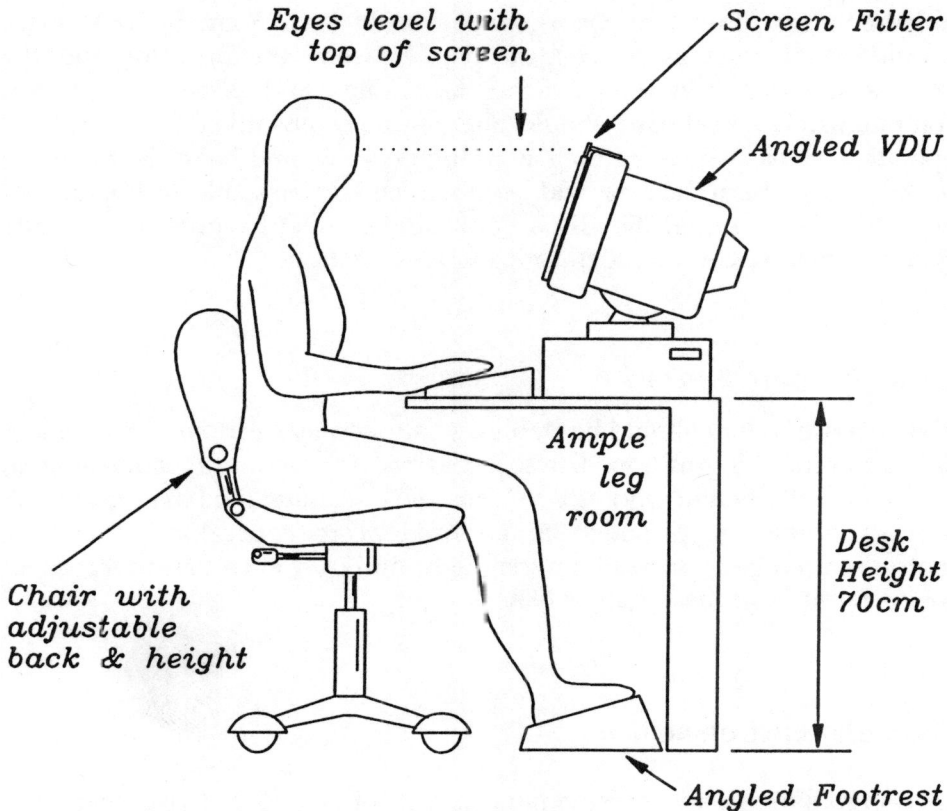

**Figure 6.3** VDU operator ergonomics

magnetic emissions by around 98 per cent. Cheaper filters will only reduce glare, which whilst relieving eyestrain in the short term will have no impact on static and radiation-linked complaints such as cataract formation and health risks to the unborn during pregnancy.

The characters on the monitor display should be well defined, of adequate size and with adequate spacing between lines. Screen brightness and contrast should be under operator control, and the image should be stable with no flickering or instability.

## Desk height, keyboard and leg room

The desk should be 70 cm high, with ample leg room available beneath (some 'workstation' PC desks offer no leg room whatsoever and are unsuitable for other than occasional use). At least 5 cm of desk space should be allowed as a wrist support between the operator and the keyboard, which can reduce aches and pains and possibly even RSI complaints. The keyboard should also be freely positionable, so that the operator can easily change their working position, and have clear legends upon its keys. Both the desk and keyboard should be stable and made of a non-reflective material. Finally a copy holder must be provided if copy typing forms part of the operator's job specification.

### Chair and footrest provision

The operator's chair should be stable and allow easy freedom of movement and a comfortable position. The seat and backrest should be adjustable in terms of both height and tilt to provide adequate lumbar support. A footrest should be provided to be used at the operator's discretion; footrests can relieve pressure on the thighs and may even be surfaced with round nodules to massage the feet.

## The wider environment

VDU ergonomics aside, more general aspects of the office environment also need to be taken into consideration. For example, room lighting must be satisfactory, providing an appropriate contrast between the screen and background environment. Reflections upon the screen or other surfaces should also be prevented – glare and bad lighting are major factors in determining levels of eyestrain and visual fatigue. Screens should therefore be positioned out of direct sunlight, all light sources should be masked, and blinds should be fitted to windows. Some writers also suggest painting the office in pastel shades to reduce reflections and glare and to improve screen-to-background contrast (King and Bone, 1989: 239).

Sufficient space must also be allowed around operator desks to permit comfortable working, and all wiring should be secured within appropriate cable ducting. Noise levels should also be minimized, which may require acoustic hoods being placed over frequently used impact printers. Rest breaks are also extremely important. Most regulations suggest that the *maximum* continuous duration for screen usage should be 2 hours, and some opticians recommend 90 minutes as a maximum. The European Health and Safety Directorate recommend several frequent breaks during the working day, rather than one or two long periods away from the screen.

## The office of the future?

Finally it should be noted that office ergonomics can be concerned with more than easing computer-related occupational health concerns. Digital Equipment, for example, reports that as technology advances, individual desks and offices may become a thing of the past, making major dents in office expenditure. In Stockholm the company has created the 'office of the future' by putting aside conventional ideas about space arrangement. The environment created is open and airy, with banks of drawers for personal files and possessions, cordless telephones, mobile chairs, and computers that drop from the ceiling via height-adjustable flexibars (*Business Update*, 1993).

## Mental health and computer systems

As well as inducing physical health complaints, the spread of computers and other forms of information technology across the workplace has lead to the definition of various associated mental health conditions. These most commonly result from a fear of, and hence resistance to, new forms of technology.

### Technostress and technology resistance

The introduction of any computer system will impact both formally and informally upon patterns of work activity within the office. Formally, job specifications, responsibilities and perhaps communications patterns will be altered, whilst informally work groups will find their norms, power and status redefined. Many people simply do not like change and thus may resist it regardless. Others may feel that their job is threatened or downgraded – managers, for example, now 'forced' to use keyboards that were once 'only typed-upon by their secretary'. Still other employees may feel ignorant and embarrassed at their lack of computer literacy, leading to low levels of self-esteem. Finally some workers may feel that they have simply become pawns of the computer, or possibly that computers will just intensify management control. (The latter is perhaps a very real fear, with managers frequently being able to monitor measures such as the keystrokes executed per hour for each VDU operator.)

All of the above factors may lead to **technostress** – a physical and emotional burnout resulting from a person's inability to cope with new technology (Timm et al., 1990: 392). Some writers also talk of **cyberphobia** in describing extreme cases of technostress where people show classical phobia symptoms such as dizziness or high blood pressure attributed solely to their hatred or fear of computers (Capron and Perron, 1993: 5).

## Technostress responses

Three common responses to technostress are *aggression*, *projection* and *avoidance*. The aggressive response may be to become verbally abusive, or perhaps even physically to attack a computer to render it inoperable. Thankfully, the projection response is far more common, with employees blaming the system for *anything* that goes wrong in the organization. Most computer users, if being honest, will admit to having blamed mistakes, and in particular delays, on their computers. Projection perhaps allays the fear of computers: in blaming the machine, users are justifying to themselves the technology's apparent fallibility.

An avoidance response to computer technology is also common. Many people simply refuse to use a computer system if they can possibly get away with it. Undergraduates have been observed in computer labs calculating figures for an assignment on a pocket calculator before entering the numbers into a spreadsheet! Others may give up or limit their use of a computer due to frustration in attempting to fathom its operation. In his book *Culture Shock* Robert Heller (1990) notes how top executives often become *technophobic* – with many senior managers rejecting the intrusion of networked personal computers.

## Overcoming technostress

Frequently the computer-literate try and alleviate the fears and concerns of their machine-wary colleagues via logical argument. They may, for example, cite the cost and efficiency benefits of a new system. This approach will rarely reduce technostress levels, as it does nothing to allay emotional concerns regarding the impact of technology. A four-step approach to reducing technostress levels with more chance of success is suggested by Callahan and Fleenor (1987), who note that managers should:

- take the lead by using computers themselves to demonstrate their merits;
- encourage and reward employees who show an interest in computers;
- establish a PC training centre where interested employees can experiment; and
- provide thorough employee computer training.

Like any other workplace symptom, technostress will only become a significant organizational problem if it is left unaddressed. If it is recognized and steps are taken in an attempt to alleviate the condition, then technostress becomes a *feedback signal* leading to more positive and enlightened computer system operations. As noted at the start of this chapter, computers cause problems for people and organizations. It is the manager's job to turn such problems around into positive solutions.

## Summary

Developing and implementing a computer system can be a frustrating and drawn-out process. In is therefore important to remain positive, with coherent planning and upbeat communications to instill commitment to change across the organization. Even when computer systems are installed and working, their very existence may cause employee concerns, especially in the field of occupational health. Today, if only for legal reasons, managers must be aware of these fears and react accordingly.

Specifically this chapter has:

- Stressed the importance and the role of planning, people and communications in achieving new system success.
- Introduced the six-phase systems development lifecycle, together with other development/implementation methodologies.
- Indicated the importance of office ergonomics and occupational health concerns.
- Summarized common health complaints, together with EC requirements and suggestions for their alleviation.
- Discussed technophobia and technology resistance.

## Review and discussion exercise

Clement Dozzle is the owner and manager of a medium-sized firm of accountants, and has read that a similar competitor has recently been taken to court by an employee regarding several computer-related occupational health hazards. Although at present his company does not use computers, Mr Dozzle is to recommend an extensive programme of computerization in the near future. He has therefore asked you to prepare a report on the matter. In particular, Mr Dozzle would like answers to the following questions:

1. It is likely that any employees will attempt to sue him when and if a computer system is installed, and if so on what grounds?
2. When any new computer system is introduced, what forms of resistance to its implementation may Clement expect from his employees?
3. Can the development and implementation of any computer system be managed so as to curtail any potential problems concerning occupational health or technology resistance?
4. Would it be more advisable simply to abandon the idea of installing any computer equipment altogether?

# 7 Computer security, data integrity and related legislation

To a large degree, the development of business computing has been concerned with making vast quantities of processed information readily available in an easy-to-access fashion. Most technological developments and moves towards improved human–computer interaction conjure up nightmares for those charged with the security of information and other corporate resources. For the more widespread and user-friendly information technology becomes, the more vulnerable the data stored and processed within computer systems becomes. Threats to the integrity of the data on which so many companies rely may arise quite accidentally. An employee who inadvertently miskeys information or deletes a file can cause just as much havoc as the computer hacker intent on industrial sabotage. This chapter reviews computer security together with the techniques that may be employed to minimize the range of threats to which business systems are exposed. It also highlights key computer-related legislation in the United Kingdom.

## Security perceptions

All managers should be aware of the problems inherent in securing information systems and computer-controlled resources across modern organizations. It is also important to appreciate that computer security is not just concerned with the control of, and access to, potentially valuable information. It is also concerned with the security of actual resources, most notably money. All banks and financial markets move and store money within vast, networked computer systems. In the 1990s money itself is a virtual, electronic phenomena. Figures held in computers may also represent physical items, e.g. component inventory levels in stock control systems. If computer systems are not adequately protected, then the modern species of electronic criminal will find it much easier to pilfer a far wider range of ill-gotten gains than his swag-bag swinging compatriot of old.

Within this chapter computer security will be broadly defined. Any threat to the integrity of the data within a computer, or unauthorized data access, will be taken as a security risk. Data integrity threats resulting from unintentional employee actions, system failures and natural causes will also be addressed.

Potential security problem areas are still narrowly perceived by many organizations. Hospitals, for example, may only be concerned with patient privacy, banks with the integrity of electronic account balances, and government bodies with risks posed by terrorists or sabotage. Almost all organizations, however, are vulnerable to a wide range of computer-related security threats.

## Banks and security standards

Standards for computer security across industry have been primarily determined by banks and other financial institutions. The 'if this security method is safe enough for financial purposes, it's good enough for us' idea still widely prevails. Unfortunately, banks and financial institutions have not been at the forefront of computer technology. They are also concerned with an entirely different set of vulnerabilities than those prominent in the corporate environment. It has therefore been noted that:

> Computer banking security is, at best, minimally acceptable for banking . . . [where] . . . embezzlement is usually the greatest perceived threat to computer security. . . . [and thus] Comprehensive control of the privileges of the users and detailed audit trails are reasonable security features to handle this threat. (Weiss, 1992: 445)

In other words, banks are primarily concerned with ensuring that only authorized personnel are able to *alter* their data, and with knowing *who* has made changes should they occur. Many business organizations may be more concerned that unauthorized users should not be able to *access* their systems, and hence their market analysis, strategic plans or technical expertise. Similarly, if a mistake occurs in a banking system (such as an incorrect account debit), it may cause customer annoyance, but the error may be safely rectified after any complaint has arisen. In contrast, corruptions in data concerning the medication for a hospital patient could prove fatal. It is therefore clear than different organizations will have different security and data integrity priorities. Reliance on banking security procedures and technology is simply not prudent across industry as a whole.

## Threats to data integrity and computer security

There are a great many ways in which the integrity or security of computer data or physical resources may be threatened, relating to both unintentional and malicious or hostile events. Despite popular misconceptions, the majority of threats to the integrity of computer operations result from mishaps during internal organizational activities, rather than from hostile external involvement (Parker, 1976). Kenneth Weiss (1992) suggests that there are seven forms of computer-system vulnerability to which most organizations may be exposed: error, embezzlement, ego (hacker attack), eavesdropping, espionage, enmity (sabotage) or extortion. Whilst these 'seven Es' provide a handy checklist against which potential loopholes in most computer systems can be gauged, they are not necessarily exhaustive. A more complete categorization of threats to computer security and data integrity may include:

- operator error;
- hardware failures;
- software bugs;
- hacker attack;
- viruses, worms, trojans and logic bombs;
- hardware theft or sabotage;
- espionage, fraud or embezzlement; and
- flood, fire and natural disasters.

### *Operator error*

The potential for accidental operator error to corrupt the integrity of computer data is frequently ignored. A common mistake may simply involve the inaccurate keying of one digit in a stock or account code, or the addition of an extra zero on the end of a monetary balance. Feedback loops and checksums can be built into most systems to minimize the effects of such occurrences. For example, once a stock code is keyed into an order system, the name of the item in question may be displayed. If this is incorrect, the user has a feedback to indicate their entry error. Similarly, producing checksums of numerical entries entered in batches can serve as a guide to detecting errors in data accuracy and magnitude.

Keying errors aside, PC users in particular may also accidentally erase valuable data files. Whilst in theory this problem may be overcome via education so that users fully understand the operation of their system, in practice we all accidentally delete or corrupt files from time to time. Maintaining multiple back-ups of important files is therefore a prudent safety measure to minimize the consequences of unintentional file erasure.

## *Hardware failures*

Hardware mishaps can also lead to serious, and sometimes unnoticed, corruptions of computer data. If a PC *crashes* (locks-up and ceases to function) its user's most recent work will probably be lost and data files stored on its hard disk may be corrupted. Brief power fluctuations are the most common cause of hardware failure and subsequent data loss or corruption. Faulty data media may also lead to data being lost or corrupted. Purchasing a **surge protector** to isolate a computer from variances in mains power may alleviate problems with the former risk. Risks pertaining to the latter may be reduced by purchasing only quality computer disks branded from a reputable manufacturer.

## *Software bugs*

Mistakes in the program coding or specification of computer software (termed *bugs* after the insect that once jammed a punched-card reader) may lead to data corruption and even financial losses. Whereas entry errors may be largely avoided by feedbacks and checksums, and back-ups can secure against accidental file erasure or corruption, software faults can go undetected for months. An expensive example concerns the *SABRE* reservation system introduced at American Airlines in 1987. The software was supposed to increase company profits by automatically adjusting the number of discounted seats on certain flights. Unfortunately it erroneously reported no discounted seats on many flights, and passengers subsequently took cheaper seats on other airlines. In a three-month period the programming error cost American Airlines an estimated \$50m (Rochester and Rochester, 1991: 247).

Software errors of this magnitude serve not only to indicate the extent of our reliance on computer systems today, but also the necessity for rigorous system specification and testing (as discussed in the last chapter). They also signal why top programmers may increasingly command extremely high salaries.

The wish to avoid errors may also explain why cheap versions of standard software packages do not sell well in business. A company may save a few hundred pounds purchasing a cheap program, but may loose thousands if an unidentified bug within it wreaks even minor havoc with their data. Cheap software is just not worth the risk, with price being second to trusted operational accuracy and reliability for most organizations.

## Hacker attack!

A hacker is somebody who gains unauthorized access to a computer system, frequently via the telephone system. This access may be for purposes of espionage, fraud or embezzlement (as discussed later), although many hackers gain entry to systems simply to have fun and satisfy their own ego. In doing so, however, they may corrupt data and endanger vital operations.

Hackers rose to prominence in the 1980s as personal computers with modems became widespread. Several 'bored' home computer users (typically male adolescents) whiled away the midnight hours breaking into large corporate and even defence systems, including those of NASA, NATO and the Pentagon. Today hacking for 'fun' is not such a problem, largely because the original hacker generation highlighted many deficiencies in computer security that have subsequently been tightened up.

## Viruses, worms, trojans and logic bombs

Whereas bugs in software coding are unintentional mistakes, **computer viruses** and associated programs (like 'worms', 'trojans' and 'logic bombs') are deliberately created by manic individuals to corrupt computer operations. As with many hacker system violations, most viruses are conceived for ego purposes, perhaps because hackers have no means of access into stand-alone PC systems. Viruses are usually passed from machine to machine via 'infected' floppy disks.

The first computer virus 'attack' was recorded on 22 October 1987 at the University of Delaware. It infected hundreds of floppy disks and destroyed at least one student's thesis (Clough and Mungo, 1992: 85). Like many viruses that have followed, the so named 'Brain' virus was programmed to replicate across all disks inserted into a computer by accessing their *boot sector*. This portion of the disk effectively controls disk storage operations, meaning that its corruption can render a disk useless.

Today, there are hundreds of known computer viruses, most of which can be detected by *anti-virus software*. To allay a popular fear, it should be noted that computer hardware itself is never damaged when a computer becomes virus infected. Thus, removing the power wipes any virus strains from a PC's memory, although not from its internal hard disk, to which most viruses will copy themselves. Sometimes anti-virus software can *clean* infected floppy or hard disks. In more severe circumstances, hard disks will require reformatting after an acute virus attack (a task *definitely* reserved for a computer expert). Virus-infected floppy disks are best discarded.

The terms 'worm', 'trojan' and 'logic bomb' are now used to describe particular forms of maliciously created computer programs of the virus genre. A **worm** is a program that takes up residence in a computer's memory, and then reproduces to cause the system to slow down or even crash, ceasing operations altogether.

A **trojan** (named after the Greek wooden horse) is a little program that tempts a user to execute it on their system. The first trojan arrived with a piece of electronic mail stating that users should run the program to 'enjoy themselves!' When they did, a christmas tree was drawn on their screen. Unbeknown to the users, whilst drawing the christmas tree image the trojan program also located their electronic address file and mailed itself to thousands upon thousands of other computers. Trojans are effectively electronic chain-letters, and not true viruses, as they rely on 'invited' user execution to spread through computer networks.

Finally, we have the most dangerous species of malicious computer program: the **logic bomb**. Logic bombs do not replicate and are designed to lie dormant within a computer until some preprogrammed date or receipt of a special instruction. They then 'explode' – deleting or modifying files, erasing the hard disk, and perhaps spreading a virus, worm or trojan to other computer systems.

### Hardware theft or sabotage

In the days of the mainframe, the computer equipment in most organizations was housed in a highly secure facility. With the spread of PCs and other downsized hardware, most computers and other hardware items no longer enjoy location-specific security. The theft or vandalism of computer equipment from large organizations is unfortunately now commonplace. Especially in large, open-plan offices where staff turnover may be high and IT personnel may regularly be installing or removing equipment. As Roberts notes, in such an environment:

> A brazen criminal could arrive and very probably get staff to help load equipment onto a trolley and take it away. . . . A laser printer was only noticed to be missing from County Hall when an inventory was done. Its whereabouts unknown and no one with any memory of someone collecting, or even moving it. It was just assumed that the equipment had been moved to another location where it was needed.   (Roberts, 1992: 26).

Of course when computer hardware is stolen, the data on any internal disk devices goes along with it. The theft of portable computer equipment can be particularly worrying in this respect, as portable machines are often used by senior personnel – and therefore often store highly confidential or valuable information. The theft of a portable computer containing defence plans from a car boot during the Gulf War in 1991 is still perhaps the best example of such an offence.

## Espionage, fraud and embezzlement

Consideration of this category of security threat leads us into the murky domain of computer crime. And it is now big business. The depredations attributed to computer crime have been estimated at over £2bn per year in the United States and the United Kingdom alone – even though 85 per cent of computer crime is probably not reported (Clough and Mungo, 1992: 9). Financial institutions are the obvious targets for criminals wishing to embezzle funds via computer misuse, and the loss of business that may result from revealing that serious security breaches have occurred is too great to be risked by many such organizations. Offences committed against banks and other financial institutions are therefore unlikely to be made public if it can possibly be avoided. The value of the average computer crime has been estimated by the FBI at $400,000 (Weiss, 1992: 446).

## Flood, fire and natural disasters

Although most computer hardware is likely to be insured, the full cost of recovering data and restoring operations after a flood, fire or other natural disaster is unlikely to be reclaimed. Some large mainframe computer facilities are now housed underground in concrete bunkers, and may therefore be considered fairly safe from acts of God. These facilities, however, can still be susceptible to risks – most notably flooding from either overflowing rivers or more likely internal water sources such as burst pipes or faulty fire sprinklers. Although apparently unlikely and obscure, natural disasters do befall computer systems. The central workshops computer of Nottinghamshire County Council once had a terminal and connection port fused during a lightening storm (Roberts, 1992: 14). Perhaps little can be done to prevent similar disasters, but organizations should bear in mind that no system will ever be totally safe, and that unforeseen emergencies may therefore always be just around the corner

## Minimizing the risks

Having availed ourselves of the range of security and data integrity threats that organizations may encounter, we may consider measures that may be employed to minimize the risks faced and/or their consequences. These may be addressed under five headings:

- user authentication measures;
- physical security measures;
- back-up procedures;
- user education; and
- disaster recovery strategies.

### User authentication measures

The most common method of controlling legitimate access to a computer system, or part thereof, is via password entry. Passwords have been used for well over thirty years, with the entry of a particular phrase or code allowing an authorized user access to specified computer facilities. Password-only user authentication methods, however, can hardly be considered secure, as the code may become known to others or perhaps overcome via trial and error. For efficient **multi-factor security**, computer system access must be dependent upon verification of two of the following:

- a password;
- a token; or
- a biometric.

Whereas a password comprises a small piece of information *known* only to the user and the computer, a token (such as a credit card or key) will be uniquely *possessed*. Finally, a biometric measure (such as a fingerprint, signature, retinal pattern or voice print) will be a unique *characteristic* of an individual. Two-factor security is far more difficult to overcome than one-factor, as it relies on possession or being something as well as simply knowing a piece of information. Common examples are found in banking systems. To obtain money from a cashpoint ATM, a customer needs to insert both a credit card (a token) and a password (or personal identification number). Similarly, credit card sales are usually validated via a signature, as are paper cheques.

Implementing two-factor computer security systems can prove prohibitively expensive, as most hardware has no provision to read tokens such as credit cards or keys, or biometric patterns such as fingerprints or retinal patterns. One emerging solution to this may involve the use of electronic *smartcards* as tokens that display codes unique to their individual owner: 'The card would be designed to change its visual display automatically with every use, and a synchronised host computer would be programmed to accept the card's displayed code only whilst it was being displayed' (Weiss, 1992: 447). The card could also be constructed to 'self-destruct' upon tampering, providing a counterfeit-resistant token to be used in conjunction with a password. No hardware additions would be needed to install the system, but two-factor security would become possible with each user entering a password and their present smartcard code to gain system access.

## Physical security measures

As already noted, although mainframe and minicomputer hardware is likely to be secure by virtue of its location, personal computer hardware can be easy to pilfer. From the criminal's point of view, most PC equipment possesses the desirable properties of being expensive, portable and homogeneous. There is nothing that can be done about the former, so organizations need to address the latter two hardware features in addition to appraising their building security systems.

With regard to portability, various locking plates can now be purchased through which steel chains or wires are interlaced to prevent equipment being removed. Although of no deterrent to the professional, cutter-endowed criminal, these devices will protect against opportunists and 'casual burglars.' Clearly marking computer equipment with machine numbers, codes or company logos will also reduce the risk of theft. Selling a stolen PC with a six-inch, logo-emblazoned metal plate epoxyed to its casing can hardly be the dream of most criminals! Both hardware marking and securing it with cabling plates is relatively inexpensive compared to the replacement of even one printer, monitor or PC. Some computer manufacturers, most notably Apple, are now making the process easier by forging security rings to the back of their equipment through which a chain or locking cable may be passed.

### Back-up procedures

If only one message is to be patterned into cranial matter from reading this chapter then it has to be **always keep at least two copies of *all* files, preferably three, and preferably across more than one location**. Users of word processors will usually back-up their own data to multiple floppy disks. A typical back-up procedure for a PC network will involve using a tape streamer to copy hard disk files from the central server to data cartridges. A common 'back-up cycle' involves using six tapes. Just one day's work will be backed-up on a separate tape from Monday through to Thursday, with the same four tapes being used each week. On Friday, the entire hard disk will be backed-up to one of the two remaining tapes used alternately. This system renders a high level of data security – providing, of course, that the data cartridges used are clearly labelled and securely stored. A fireproof safe may be prudently employed for data cartridge storage.

### User education

Given the range of risks to which organizations may be exposed, it is perhaps surprising that the managers made responsible for the security of computer systems are often overburdened, underbudgeted and largely unaware of the technical issues involved. As far as computer security is concerned, education still has a major role to play across all levels of most organizations. Many employees are far more interested in user friendliness and computer access rather than security hazards. They may often ignore security and back-up procedures, seeing them simply as work inhibitors.

For example, few employees would leave confidential files lying idly on their desks when away from the office – especially if they were located near a photocopier. In contrast, many people leave floppy disks containing similar information unprotected, and typically next to a PC in which they may easily be copied. Similarly employees frequently do not logout of company networks during breaks from the keyboard. Many users therefore need to be woken up to the potential for industrial espionage within the modern workplace. Most information held on computers is very easy to steal compared to that stored in paper files, if only in terms of its low bulk-to-storage ratio. Several bad habits also need clearing up – such as selecting simple-to-figure passwords like the name of a spouse, and worse still writing passwords on notes attached to VDU screens! Many organizations now have strict rules on permissable password lexicons from which all words with obvious links to their user are banned. Passwords are typically also changed every three months. In many organizations it is also forbidden to use a non-company floppy disk for fear of virus infection.

## *A disaster recovery strategy*

All organizations should have some form of disaster recovery strategy detailing actions to be taken in the event of large-scale system failures. These strategies will include details for the recovery of data from back-up media. They may also involve invoking facilities for emergency power should an electricity failure occur. Where system failure would be disastrous, organizations may physically duplicate essential components on-site as back-ups in case of an emergency. Less costly measures may involve reciprocal agreements between firms using compatible hardware to offer mutual support if either firm has a disaster. Alternatively a **hot-site agreement** may be offered by a computer dealer whereby compatible system hardware will be made available if required in an emergency. Where such agreements cannot be forged with suppliers, commercial computer bureau may be contracted to provide standby facilities should the need arise.

## Computer-related legislation

In the United Kingdom there are two items of computer-related legislation of which organizations should be aware. The first, the **Data Projection Act (1984)**, is primarily concerned with protecting the rights of those on whom computer records are held. It is therefore a piece of legislation with which all organizations must comply. The second significant act, the **Computer Misuse Act (1990)**, provides legal powers to protect computer systems themselves against criminal activity. In contrast to the Data Protection Act, the Computer Misuse Act is more likely to be encountered by organizations in the prosecution of parties acting to their detriment.

## The Data Protection Act (1984)

The Data Protection Act (DPA) established two main principles concerning the storage and use of computer information held on living individuals:

- The right of an individual to obtain a copy of any information held upon them, and to challenge the validity of that information and if appropriate claim compensation resulting from its inaccuracy or misuse.
- The obligation for computer users to be open about the use of data upon their systems and to ensure that all data is accurate and secure.

Control of those who store and use information held upon individuals is provided by a system of registration, with penalties for either failing to register or acting beyond the scope of registration. With some exceptions, companies must therefore register all records held on computer with the **Data Protection Registrar**. It is important to remember that this applies whether the data is held on a mainframe system or simply a stand-alone PC in the corner of the office. Exceptions for data registration relate mainly to information pertaining to national security, certain payroll and accounts data, domestic information, and information required by law to be made available to the public (Bainbridge, 1990: 191).

From an individual's point of view, the main problem with the DPA is that they can only request a copy of information held on them when they know somebody is holding it. This may sound obvious, but people blacklisted for credit, for example, may not know the source of the information used in judgement against them.

## The Computer Misuse Act (1990)

The Computer Misuse Act (CMA) widened computer law to protect computers, programs and data in addition to individual rights as covered in the DPA. Three levels of offence are included:

- unauthorized access to computer material;
- unauthorized access with intent to commit or facilitate commission of further offences; and
- unauthorized modification of computer material.

Hacking into computer systems is illegal under the first two provisions of the CMA, with the penalty for unauthorized access with intent to commit further offences carrying a potential penalty of up to five years imprisonment. A side-effect of the last clause of the CMA also provides legal redress against those who create and spread computer viruses, since writing a program that impairs the operation of any computer becomes an offence (Rockman, 1990: 171).

## Copyright and software theft

In addition to the DPA and CMA, an additional piece of legislation for all computer users to bear in mind is the *Copyright Designs and Patents Act (1988)*. This replaced the previous *Copyright (Computer Software) Amendment Act (1985)*, ensuring the principle that any software owner should be the sole beneficiary of the sale, copying or use of that software. In other words, software piracy is theft. If you need five copies of a popular word processor package, then you must buy five copies, or a license to cover the same.

The only software exempt or partially exempt from illegal copying is known as **public domain** (PD) or **shareware**. PD software is created for personal fulfilment by computer enthusiasts, and may be freely copied and distributed. Shareware programs may also be freely copied. If found useful, however, a shareware fee becomes payable to the owner, details for the submission of which will accompany the software. In the United Kingdom, many users fail to send in their shareware fee (usually ranging from between £5 and £30), which is a pity as it discourages the creation of this genre of often high-quality 'try-before-you-buy' software.

## Summary

Most computer systems and the data within them are at risk from a variety of potential threats, both internal and external to the organization, and both unintentional and malicious. Cost will always be a factor when implementing computer security measures. Even when no financial barriers are imposed, system operations and data integrity can not be guaranteed, as demonstrated by computer failures associated with the US Space Shuttle or Apollo space missions. Organizations will always need to strike a balance between cost and system risk-exposure. The most effective procedures to guard against security risks are also frequently the most simple: locks on doors; regular back-ups stored in fireproof safes or at alternative locations; careful enforcement of password definition; and most importantly user education.

Specifically, chapter 7 has addressed:

- The narrow perception of security and data integrity threats by most users.
- The range of vulnerabilities likely to be faced by computer systems and data.
- Measures that may be taken to minimize computer-related risks, including authentication methods, back-up procedures and user education.
- Computer-related legislation.

## Review and discussion questions

1. What disasters could befall the computer system of an organization of which you are aware?
2. What measures could be employed to minimize these risks, and to allow operations to continue should they occur?

# 8 Towards the future . . .

Good managers tend to be proactive, planning visions for the future rather than reacting to happenings as they occur. To wet the appetite of eager forward planners, this chapter provides a brief summary of some of the developments that may impact on business computer application in the near future. Technology continues to evolve, and although high-specification networked PCs running current application genres will continue to play a prominent role in organizational and personal functioning, so too will emerging softwares and hardwares such as multimedia, expert systems and personal digital assistants. Dynamic organizational forms are increasingly feasible due to advances in computing and telecommunications technology. The dream of artificial intelligence will also one day be realized, and the new medium of cyberspace may become widely accessible with mind-blowing possibilities for future business development. As we approach the third millennia, a fifth generation of computer hardware is finally being realized. For those who see information technology as a blessing to mankind, the best is definitely yet to come.

## Looking ahead

Predicting the future of computing development is an occupation at which many writers have failed. In general we may expect hardware to become smaller and more powerful, software to become more user friendly, communications difficulties to be increasingly overcome, and the price of everything to tumble. More specifically, it is probable that future screen displays will be based upon flat LCD technology rather than CRT monitors. This will not only save on space, but perhaps more significantly will curtail any risks associated with high-voltage radiation in the office. Credit-card sized PCMCIA solid-state storage devices and smartcards will also proliferate, as will new optical disk technologies. Although the days of the floppy disk are unlikely to be numbered, in ten years time they may well not be the dominant form of non-fixed computer storage.

## The green machine

Environmental concerns already being voiced are likely to raise questions concerning the power consumption of all forms of computer hardware. The shift from CRT to LCD displays will almost certainly lead to reduced electricity consumption. Widespread utilization of power-saving circuitry designed to switch off internal components when not in operation may also greatly cut computer power requirements. Such circuitry is already widely employed in portable computers where battery life is at a premium. Considering that most computers spend most of their powered-up lives waiting for human instructions, it is perhaps surprising that energy-saving features are not yet commonplace. Aside from saving fossil fuels and reducing pollution, decreasing the power consumption of computers will also save business organizations tens of millions of pounds per annum.

## Key new developments

Certain currently juvenile technologies and software forms can already be identified as likely to take lead roles in business computer applications in the near future. The compilation of the following list can at best be arbitrary. In the time it has taken for this book to come to press several significant new developments in business computing will have occurred. Still others, at the time of writing of great importance, will have been superseded by fresh invention and imagination. The six specific areas of development to be detailed in this chapter, however, will almost certainly still be receiving popular business attention in the years and even decades ahead. Specifically, discussion will therefore now be focused upon developments pertaining to:

- multimedia;
- expert systems;
- artificial intelligence;
- personal digital assistants;
- dynamic organizational forms; and
- the technology of cyberspace.

## Multimedia: the new killer application?

Computer manufacturers and software publishers are always looking for new applications with which to make another tidy fortune. Many believe that **multimedia** constitutes the next 'killer application' for the picking, with the computer press at times saturated with glossy coverage of this relatively new area. But just what is multimedia, and perhaps more importantly, what will be its implications for the business user?

### *Integration and interaction*

Multimedia basically involves the harmonious integration of text, computer graphics and high-quality sound. Because of the large volumes of data necessary to produce high-quality graphics and computer animation, most multimedia systems utilize CD-ROM for data storage. Dedicated multimedia systems, such as the Philips **CD-I** and Commodore's **CDTV**, are designed to educate and entertain users. Typical software packages include games and simulations, a world atlas, medical dictionaries and illustrated encyclopedias. Most applications can be accessed interactively by the user. Click on the name 'Bach' in a multimedia encyclopedia, for example, and a picture of the composer will appear accompanied by the dulcet tones of one of his musical creations.

### *Multimedia standards*

Due to the vast array of differing PC graphics and other hardware configurations, the Multimedia PC Marketing Council has laid down a basic specification for the hardware required to run multimedia applications on an IBM PC. Many suppliers now conform to this standard, with 'multimedia PCs' coming equipped with at least a 386 CPU, at least VGA graphics, a CD-ROM drive and sound card such as the SoundBlaster II. Most modern PCs may be upgraded to this multimedia standard by simply adding a CD-ROM drive and sound card. They will then be able to access the ever-increasing range of CD-ROM multimedia titles now available.

*Multimedia in business*

Multimedia is most likely to be used in the business world for training purposes. Because of the potential for user interaction, information retention after a multimedia training session is usually high. Multimedia-based training is likely to be far less expensive for the organization, and far more enjoyable for the participant, than traditional off-job delivery mechanisms such as formal lectures. Although hyped with an 'enthusiasm bordering on the evangelical' (Goodwins, 1991), multimedia is unlikely to be used for many business applications other than employee education in the foreseeable future. More likely, the closer integration of audio, graphical and lexical data forms will simply permit more user-attractive interfaces to be created for other genres of software. The only major impact of the technology for most business users will be the growing acceptance of CD-ROM drives as standard items of kit over the next five years. Indeed, with the increasing size of many common software packages, and low reproduction costs, the CD-ROM may eventually replace the floppy disk as the major software and information supply media.

## Expert systems: encoding our knowledge

The developments in high-capacity, low-cost storage technology and interactive user interfaces that have enabled multimedia development will also permit the widespread creation and adoption of knowledge-based systems. Such **expert systems** are designed to provide assistance in problem solving and data analysis in narrow disciplines such as geological surveying, medical diagnosis or financial planning. The systems are programmed with a set of rules (or *heuristics*) pertaining to the field in question, in addition to having access to a vast data set (or *knowledge base*) of past cases. A medical expert system, for example, may ask for the details of any symptoms suffered by a patient and use these to formulate a diagnosis of their likely condition. Similarly, a geological surveying system may take satellite data and predict the likely location of oil or other natural resources. The general structure of an expert system is represented in figure 8.1.

Most expert systems feature a human-friendly interface so that they may be accessed by users who are not computer experts. The user interface links the user to the system's *inference engine* within which the system's heuristic

```
        ┌─────────────┐
        │    END      │
        │    USER     │
        └─────────────┘
               ↕
        ┌─────────────┐
        │    USER      │
        │  INTERFACE   │
        └─────────────┘
               ↕
┌─────────────┐        ┌─────────────┐
│  INFERENCE  │ ←────→ │  KNOWLEDGE  │
│   ENGINE    │        │    BASE     │
└─────────────┘        └─────────────┘
```

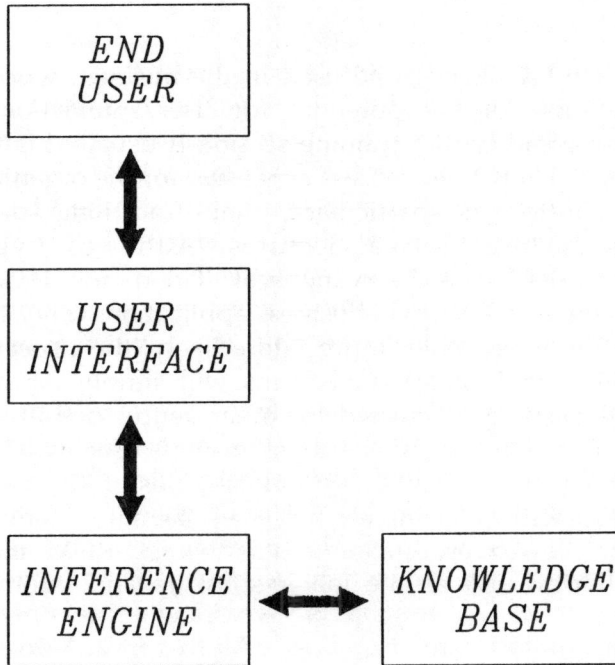

**Figure 8.1**    The structure of an expert system

routines are applied with reference to the knowledge base. An expert system may be viewed as possessing 'intelligence' in a specialist field, and indeed developments in this area are at present the most promising in the diverse research arena of 'artificial intelligence'.

## Artificial intelligence: dream or reality?

**Artificial intelligence** (AI) is concerned with the creation of computer hardware and software systems with the ability to synthesize aspects of human behaviour or cognition. In a very real sense, AI is attempting to automate processes of human judgement, such as decision making, that have previously only been augmentable. Most research is currently directed towards the computer comprehension of natural spoken or written language, vision-processing systems, and automated decision making. Inevitably, AI developments also stray into disciplines as diverse as robotics, philosophy and cognitive psychology.

## The Turing test

In 1950 Alan Turing coined a now famous benchmark by which to gauge success in synthesizing computer intelligence. A subject is seated at a screen and keyboard used for two-way communication. They then type their half of a 'conversation' on the keyboard, whilst the contributions of another (unseen) party to the discussion appear on the VDU screen. AI is deemed to have been achieved when the subject involved is unable to distinguish whether they are in communication with another person also sitting at a terminal, or are actually conversing with a computer. In other words, the computer needs to be able to convince its subject that it possesses human intelligence.

Clearly computers will need to be able to comprehend natural language if they are to pass the Turing test. Despite numerous attempts, a system that can pass the test and fool *every* subject into thinking that they are communicating with a person has yet to be created. A natural language program called ELIZA has arguably come closest, and has fooled many users into believing they are communicating with a human being rather than a machine. Indeed some subjects have become emotionally attached to ELIZA, feeling comforted by its 'advice'. All that ELIZA does, however, is to scan for key words in conversation. These are then used to trigger responses, which often involve turning a query back into another question. Thus even when ELIZA appears intelligent it has no comprehension of either its subject's inputs or its own responses.

Rapid developments in the 1950s and 1960s led many to believe that artificial intelligence would be rapidly achieved. After all, in little over twenty years computers had developed from simply calculating ballistics tables to actually beating humans at chess. Unfortunately the conception of AI still eludes humanity. Some have even labelled true AI 'unattainable' and shifted to other arenas of study.

## Synthesizing the obvious

The problem, at first peculiar, is that whereas it is fairly easy to encode narrow but complex cognitive processes into software routines (as in expert systems), apparently 'simple' mental tasks – engaging in a social conversation about the weather, for example, or commenting on events in the latest smash soap opera – have proved near-impossible to synthesize. The problem in getting computers to comprehend what we as humans have evolved to find obvious stems from the fact that our language tends to be both ambiguous and highly context specific. Imagine how a man walking down a railway carriage, pointing to a clearly unoccupied seat, and asking a nearby passenger if anybody was sitting there, would confuse an artificial mind! To a human being the question makes perfect sense, for the man is really asking if anybody *has* been sitting there, and thus may return to occupy the seat in the immediate future. Encoding such language subtleties based around shared contextual understandings into computer systems has proved extremely difficult. The rules for social interplay are incredibly complex. Even the rules relating to the natural world are difficult to encode. Asked to build a tower, no toddler would commence by placing the top brick in mid air, yet to a computer unaware of gravity, the positioning of the uppermost block may seem the obvious starting point.

The achievement of machine intelligence will probably defeat our best research teams for a few more decades to come. Increased memory capacities and processing technologies, however, will surely one day allow the rules and heuristics relating to the world and human interaction to be encoded into a computer system. At some point computers will become intelligent. Computer assistants may then take on tasks for which you now employ human beings. Although as one writer concerned with the future of mankind notes:

> Despite the growing power of computers, we are not moving towards the human-like robots of science fiction. What, other than the novelty, would be the value of integrating generalised human capabilities into a robot that could mimic human behaviour? An intelligent computer companion would be cheaper and more useful if it were pocket-size rather than clunking alongside us in a humanoid frame.   (Stock, 1993: 44)

Surprisingly, a new race of computer devices to aid our work and play and now with us. Lacking familiar keyboards and disk drives, these devices are usually referred to as 'personal digital assistants'.

## Personal digital assistants: new friends in our pockets?

A **personal digital assistant** (PDA) is a small but powerful keyboard-less computer and communications device operated with a pen by writing and drawing on its pressure-sensitive screen. The first PDAs are now on sale after five years of joint development between Apple and Sharp, and made possible due to the development of higher-density silicon chips. Sharp's

PDA is currently called the *Expert Pad*, and the first of Apple's machines the *Newton Messagepad*.

PDAs are much more than fancy electronic organizers, although having roughly the dimensions of an A5 rectangle and being under an inch thick they are about the same size. Most of the top surface is occupied by the touch-sensitive LCD screen used for both pen input and output display. Connectors provide a link to PC or Macintosh computers for data transfer, or to a printer or computer network. Long-term storage is on PCMCIA cards that slot into the top of the hardware.

## Handwriting recognition and communications

Personal digital assistants are designed to be easy to use. As a user writes on the screen their scrawl is transformed into neatly printed type. Sketches are also cleaned up into accurate drawings. The software is clever enough to know that a circle is sometimes a letter, sometimes a number, and sometimes just a circle. To delete words you can simply scrub them out and they will disappear in a puff of smoke! Unwanted documents crunch-up and fall into a trash can.

PDAs are *personal* because they learn from their owner the more they are used. Individual handwriting recognition therefore improves over time. The software also understands as well as recognizes certain words such as 'call', 'meet' and 'remember': 'If you tap the Assist icon and then write 'call Mum' the Newton will look up your mother's phone number and dial it for you' (Wilson, 1993).

Communications from current PDAs depend on the unit being linked into a computer network or internet via a tiny fax modem. The user can send messages at any time, however, and the machine will store them up for automatic transmission as soon as it is next connected to an appropriate outlet. Future Newton PDAs will have communications devices built in. A whole new age of computer-enabled communications will then dawn. As Michael Tchao, manager of the Newton project, enthusiastically explains:

> Imagine I'm a ski-ware salesman and I notice that one of my stores is running a little low on woolly hats – I can get out my Newton, make a quick note: 'Order Woolly Hats.' Now using the graphics capability I can sketch in the type of hat that I'd like and fax it back to my supplier. And through the wireless network the message will be sent to his fax machine. It's as simple as that.   (Hayman, 1993: 9)

## Dynamic organizational forms: children of the connectivity age?

The sale of PDAs to businessmen across the world will further increase the already rampant trend towards increased computer *connectivity*. As the *New York Times* reported in November 1991, half of the connections across the global telecommunications network already involve data communications between machines rather than spoken parlance between human beings. The ever-increasing ease of computer interconnection for communication and resource sharing now increasingly permits the existence and operation of new 'networked' forms of dynamic organization (Morgan, 1989; Daniell, 1990).

According to Morgan, 'dynamic network' organizational structures are based upon small cores of workers who 'operationalize ideas'. In the fashion industry, for example, a name and an image may be formulated by a small team of people creating a particular 'label'. This core of workers, rather than employing a large staff to bring its goods to the marketplace, instead contracts-out market surveys, product design, production and distribution to other companies, so that:

> In the public eye, the firm has a clear identity. But in reality, it is a network of firms held together by the product of the day. It changes from month to month as different ideas and products come on line, and as the core organization experiments with different partners. The firm is really a system of firms – an open-ended system of ideas and activities, rather than an entity with a clear structure and definable boundary.   (Morgan, 1989: 67)

For any production network to operate effectively, communications technologies have to be highly developed so that the core can maintain control of the activities of the agents in the marketplace contracted to perform their required functions. Networked organizations, their structural architecture constantly in a state of flux, are therefore highly dependent upon complex computer communications systems to sustain their temporal cohesion. In future, 'virtual products' designed, produced and tailored exactly to customer specifications when and where they are desired are likely to lead to 'virtual corporations' dependent on new technology for rapid environmental interaction (Davidow and Malone, 1992). Managers will need to be informed of both internal and external developments not on a weekly or daily basis, but by the hour – perhaps via PDAs communicating over wireless networks.

It is perhaps also interesting to note that in future business organizations will become more and more similar to the computer systems on which they will be dependent. This can be attributed to the fact that the network model of organizational structure:

> . . . closely resembles the physical configuration of a modern integrated information systems network. Every business unit, serving local demand, communicates extensively with other units; and every unit is guided by operating protocols, central priorities and investment decision laid down at the centre.   (Daniell, 1990: 83)

## Stepping into cyberspace: the final frontier?

As connectivity increases and transient networked forms of organizations abound, the medium of **cyberspace** will unfold offering untold possibilities for future business development. Cyberspace is the term used to refer to any virtual environment created within or between computer systems into which people may 'jack' for high-level human–computer interaction. The term was coined by novelist William Gibson, who described the medium as a 'matrix of lattices of unfolding logic' into which hackers may interface their 'disembodied consciousness' for 'consensual hallucination' (Gibson, 1984: 12). Business users may best view cyberspace as the electronic domain within their computers in which their applications programs function. Just as goldfish live in water, so computer software resides in cyberspace. Similarly all computer network communications are routed via the electronic cyberspace media.

### Cyber hardware and virtual reality

Most people are now aware of technological advances allowing complex simulations of 'real' environments via computer graphics. Architects can walk through houses before they are built. Scientists can manipulate complex molecules on their screens. Games players can tour fantasy domains. The technology of so-called **virtual reality** is rapidly advancing and becoming more commonplace, allowing people to interact within three-dimensional computer-generated environments.

The glamour hardware for virtual reality cyberspace interaction now commonly includes headsets that position stereo monitor displays before both eyes and **datagloves** that permit the wearer to move and feel objects within computer domains. Full body suits to computer-stimulate *every* physical organ are now being developed, and in a few years time we can expect computer-generated cyberspace experiences to be near-indistinguishable from events in the real world. In some instances they may be even better.

## The cyber business

The implications of virtual reality systems and cyberspace expansion for the business community may be even more staggering. Already we have noted how increased connectivity – effectively the expansion of the cyberspace created via interlinked computer networks – will and is permitting new dynamic forms of organization. Developments in technology to enable human beings to interface with computer systems can only increase this trend, permitting even more diverse corporate architectures:

> The technology will enable multidimensional, professional interaction and natural, intuitive work group formation. The technology will evolve to provide enterprises that we call Corporate Virtual Workplaces (CVWs) as highly productive replacements for current work environments. CVWs will be a key factor in the economic success of corporations in the next century. Indeed, CVWs will begin to profoundly change the character of corporations, society and our economic system.   (Pruitt and Barrett, 1991: 383)

Developments in human–computer interaction may also alter the wants of consumers and hence the nature of the products they demand. The entertainment and travel industries will almost certainly be the first to be affected. Will television, cinema and foreign holidays remain top-of-the-list leisure activities when people are able to roam fantasy cyberworlds in their own homes? How will such developments affect product marketing? And delivery mechanisms? The questions are large and as yet largely unanswered. What is certain is that the next stage of human–machine interaction will soon be with us, and that visionaries in business cannot ignore the embryonic technologies. Whilst at present the divide between the realm of human thought and reality and the electronic domain of the computer is broad (requiring complex interface technology to bring the two together), in future:

> . . . by monitoring and stimulating brain cells and also communicating with external devices, it might eventually be possible to establish complex links between computer circuitry and the human cerebral cortex. This would give

humans direct mental control over various machines and also expand mental capabilities with powerful enhancements of memory, communication and computation.   (Stock, 1993: 139–40)

## *Computer media and the next generation*

Whilst the above may seem far-fetched, a more immediate thought to bear in mind is the way in which new generations, and hence new managers and employees, will perceive the cyberspace world within computers. Everybody in business today has had to be taught (if perhaps by self-discovery) the principles of computing, graphical environments, file structures and their ilk. In the near future, we will have in residence with us an entire generation to whom the computing cybermedia has *never* had to be explicitly explained. To future children it will be as taken for granted as the two-dimensional medium of paper and marking implement. Who could honestly claim that they ever had the *concept* of marking paper to communicate and store ideas explained? Granted, you were taught to write, and probably assisted in your first drawing attempts. But the medium of writing and drawing is now an intuitive facet of human activity at this stage of our evolution. So will it be, to those to come, with the cyberspace media of computing (Barnatt, 1993). Where this will take future business organizations nobody currently in management or higher education can predict.

## Summary

Computers are becoming more and more powerful and easier to use. This final *Blueprint* chapter has discussed technologies and software forms that will lead to increased computer application, more widespread communication, and the closer and closer integration and interdependence of human beings on computer systems. Computers *are* part of our lives. As information processing and communications tools they will become more so. This trend need not be feared or resisted. Early man forged his tools from wood and stone and twine. Over hundreds of thousands of years of evolution we have simply come to fashion ours from plastic, metal and semiconductor materials. The final words I will leave to Stock, author of the thought-provoking *Metaman*, and to Bill Gates of the giant software corporation Microsoft:

The full potential of electronic processing is not yet clear, but there is no reason to believe its capabilities will not eventually far surpass those of the human brain.   (Stock, 1993: 41)

Certainly computers will be in any meaningful sense as smart as people at some point. It's turned out to be a very hard problem and it'll still take some time. But we will get there – there's no secret source that the old chips won't be able to deal with.   (Gates, quoted in Hayman, 1993: 6)

## Discussion exercise

Think of an organization of which you have some experience – a workplace, college or university. Then address the following questions:

1.   How may the organization's structure and operations be affected by increased computerization in the future?
2.   Which new developments will have the greatest impact?
3.   How will people react to these new developments?
4.   What problems may be encountered concerning human socialization and organizational security?

# Appendix:
# Spreadsheet tutorial exercises

## Author's note

The following exercises are intended to provide a practical, step-by-step guide to the basic operation of the *Lotus 1-2-3* spreadsheet and other compatible software packages. It is assumed that the reader will progress through the exercises whilst seated at a PC running such software. Sample 'solutions' for each exercise are listed at the end of this appendix; however, readers are encouraged not to refer to them during the exercises unless they get completely stuck. Readers with no spreadsheet or computer knowledge are advised to become familiar with the general information provided on spreadsheets in chapter 2 before continuing.

All of the following have been extensively tested in lab teaching sessions with groups of both undergraduate, MBA and short-course students, and this appendix alone is exempt from copyright so that the exercises may be copied for teaching purposes.

The exercises will work with any spreadsheet offering compatibility with *Lotus 1-2-3*, and have been tested on versions of *Lotus* itself from 2.1 upwards, as well as in *Quattro Pro* (version 3 upwards) running with the *Lotus 1-2-3* menu tree (i.e. in *Lotus 1-2-3* mode). The exercises should also work on other packages claiming total *Lotus 1-2-3 keystroke* compatabilty, such as *As-Easy-As* and *VP-Planner*, although this has not been verified by the author.

As the exercises address only the basics of spreadsheet operations, they can all quite happily be performed on the most basic of hardware running early versions of spreadsheet software. Readers using the most recent versions of *Lotus 1-2-3* or *Quattro Pro* may find that they have many more options available within program menus than referred to herein (e.g. there may be more variants of graph type that can be plotted). If this is the case, readers are encouraged to experiment with such facilities, although clearly this will lead them to diverge from the exercises as presented in this appendix.

## Important!

Please note that within the following '↵' is used to indicate when the enter/ return key on the keyboard should be pressed. This key (analogous to the carriage return key on a manual typewriter) is located on the right of the main keyboard block, and is most commonly labelled 'enter', 'return', or simply adorned with a horizontal arrow.

Secondly, note that the 'cursor' refers to the block on screen indicating where typing will appear. The cursor keys, each labelled with a small arrow in one of four directions, are thus the keys used to move the cursor around the computer screen. Also note that when editing your typing, the key marked 'del' or 'delete' is used to erase text 'below' or to the right of the cursor, whilst the key at the top right of the main keyblock (with an arrow legend) is used to erase text to the cursor's left.

Thirdly, users new to computers are recommended to avoid using the numeric keypad (on the far right of most modern keyboards), and are instead encouraged to type numbers from the top line of the main keyblock, whilst using the cursor arrow keys usually located in isolation towards the right of the keyboard. Whilst it is perfectly valid to type on the numeric keypad (on which both numbers and cursor arrows are emblazoned), the function of this keypad depends on the status of the Num(ber) Lock key, which in my experience of lab teaching has caused confusion and panic to many of those taking their first steps in computing. You have been warned!

Finally, note that the exercises that follow assume that you learn as you progress. Thus, although they initially detail every keystroke that must be made, such 'help' drops away as the exercises continue. It is thus important that you make sure that you understand why you are typing something as you progress, rather than charging blindly ahead and gaining no understanding. Good luck!

## Entering the spreadsheet program

The exercises that follow start from the assumption that you are capable of entering the spreadsheet package available on the PC before you. Access to software is obtained in a great many ways, and it is likely that many readers will be using a system presenting a simple menu allowing access to a range of different software packages. If this is the case, simply select your spreadsheet package from those on offer.

If there is no menu system, and you are simply seated at a PC displaying a DOS prompt such as:

C:\>

you will probably gain access to *Lotus 1-2-3* by typing:

CD  123  ⏎
123  ⏎

If not, you will have to address your *Lotus* manual.

Once you have entered your spreadsheet software, you are in a position to begin exercise 1.


## A note for *Quattro Pro* users

Borland's top-selling *Quattro Pro* spreadsheet runs perfectly happily as a clone of *Lotus 1-2-3*. If you are using *Quattro Pro* from a menu system, you may well be presented with an option of running it in *Lotus 1-2-3* mode, and thus you should select this option. If this is not the case, and you enter *Quattro Pro* in its native mode (with the word 'FILE' at the top left of the screen, rather than 'WORKSHEET'), press the following keys:

/    i.e. the backslash key
O    for Options
S    for Startup
M    for Menu tree
1    for 1-2-3

Your software will then operate identically to *Lotus 1-2-3* (with the word 'WORKSHEET' now appearing in the top left-hand corner).


## Exercise 1

*An introduction to spreadsheet modelling*

Once you have entered the spreadsheet program, your screen shows an area of a *worksheet* of columns (lettered) and rows (numbered). The *CELL*

*POINTER* is located in *cell* **A1**, and can be moved around the screen with the cursor/arrow keys.

The current *cell reference*, together with a record of its contents are displayed at (or just below) the top left of the screen. The 'home' key will always return the CELL POINTER to cell **A1**.

## Entering information into cells

Spreadsheet cells can hold either text, numbers or numerical expressions. To make an entry into a cell simply type on the keyboard and press <ENTER>. If you make an entry into a cell that already contains information, the new entry will replace the old one.

The following example takes you through the basics of using a spreadsheet – entering and editing data, formatting data, resizing columns, printing, saving, retrieving worksheets, and producing a graph.

## Cheers!

Bill, Fred, Kelly and Norman are drinking buddies who frequent their favourite tavern each evening. Information concerning their respective bar tabs at this establishment appears in figure A.1. You are going to enter this data into a spreadsheet, create an automatic total, alter the data, and finally produce a graph. Simply follow the steps below.

[A] Move the CELL POINTER to cell **B2**, and type: **BAR TABS** ↵
[B] Move the CELL POINTER to cell **B4**, and type **Bill** ↵
[C] Move the CELL POINTER to cell **C4**, and enter **500** ↵
[D] Continue, entering the information for Fred, Kelly and Norman, into cells **B5, C5, B6, C6, B7** and **C7**

Note that all the text you have entered has justified to the left of the cells into which it was entered, and that all the numbers have justified to the right. If you wish to make text entries (such as the names of our drinking buddies) justify to the right of a cell you can enter them with a double quote (as found on the 2 key, shifted) before them: for example entering "**Bill** into **B4**, rather than simply **Bill**. Note, however, that numerical entries (such as the bar tab values) *always* justify to the right of the cell into which they are entered. There is nothing you can or should do to prevent this – and indeed if a number is *not* justifying to the right of its cell, then it has been incorrectly entered (perhaps with a space before it), and should be entered again so that it does justify to the cell's right border.

```
        BAR TABS


        Bill                          500

        Fred                          300

        Kelly                       17.23

        Norman                         98
```

**Figure A.1**   Exercise 1: bar tab data

*Producing a total*

[E]   Enter the word **TOTAL** into cell **B9**

[F]   To make the total appear in cell **C9**, move the CELL POINTER to
      this cell and enter **+C4+C5+C6+C7**

The figure **915.23** should now appear, the spreadsheet automatically
calculating the required value. Note that you have to enter
**+C4+C5+C6+C7**, and *not* just **C4+C5+C6+C7.** If you do this, the
spreadsheet will treat your entry as text. In other words, you must
remember that when entering formulas into cells that they must always be
prefixed with a '+' sign, to indicate that they are numerical in nature.

*Editing cell entries*

Suppose that Bill paints the bar owner's office and, as payment, it is agreed
that his bar tab will be reduced by 100.

[G]   To make this alteration, move the CELL POINTER to cell **C4** and
      press the **F2** key (all the function keys are located together in a row
      at the very top of the keyboard). The contents of cell **C4** will be
      retrieved to the top left of the screen for editing. You can now use
      the cursor and delete keys to change the figure **500** to **400**. Once this
      is accomplished, simply press ↵.

Note that not only has the value in **C4** altered (from 500 to 400), but that the TOTAL has recalculated to show **815.23**

## The @SUM function

If there were a lot of customers with bar tabs in our list (say 1000), adding all the values with the formula +C4+C5+C6+ . . . etc. would take a lot of typing! To save this, spreadsheets have a very useful function called **@SUM**.

[H]   Move to **C9** and type **@SUM(C4..C7)** ↵ (do *not* include any spaces). This will replace the previous formula in **C9** – but the result will be the same. (The @ symbol is on a key on the right-hand side of the main body of the keyboard.)

When dealing with large tables of numbers, @SUM is one of the functions that make spreadsheets so powerful.

## Formatting numbers

Your spreadsheet would look neater if the numbers were all displayed to the same number of decimal places with currency signs in front of them. This is very easy to achieve with one of the many commands within the spreadsheet's command menu. At first using the menu may appear a little daunting, but you will soon get used to it, and in fact the menu is really quite user friendly.

[I]   Move to **C4**, and press / (located on the ? key, main keyblock lower right) to activate the COMMAND MENU at the top of the screen. There are several options available from the main menu (Worksheet, Range, Copy, Move and so forth), and most of these have many options available within them. Once the menu is activated, commands can be selected by simply pressing their first letter.

   The formatting command can be found within the Range option, so press **R** for Range, and you will enter another menu. You can now press **F** to select the Format option, and **C** for the Currency option. The program will then ask you to enter the number of decimal places you require. **2** is already displayed as the 'default', however, so just press ↵.

   You now have to highlight the RANGE to FORMAT. This needs to be **C4** to **C9**, displayed as **C4..C9** You can either type this, or have the program work it out for you. To make the program do the work, simply move the CELL POINTER from **C4** to **C9** – the RANGE below **C4** is highlighted and **C4..C9** is displayed at the top of the screen. Press ↵ The operation is completed! Your spreadsheet should now look much neater, with all the numbers lining up, and having currency signs before them (these will either be pound or dollar signs, depending on how your spreadsheet is set up).

## Column width changes

The bar manager has suddenly realized that he has two customers called Fred, and that as the Fred in our list is frequently inebriated, he wishes to refer to him in his records as 'Fred the Drunk'.

[J] Edit the contents of **B5** (using the **F2** key as in part [G]), and add **the Drunk** on the end of Fred's name.

You now, however, have a problem – as there is only enough room to display part of **'Fred the Drunk'** in the spreadsheet (although you can see from the cell information at the top left of the screen that the whole entry is correctly stored). To display the full entry, you thus need to make COLUMN B wider.

[K] Press **/** to activate the menu, and press **W** for Worksheet, **C** for Column and **S** for Set Width. You will see that the current column width is **9**. You can now either enter a new value, or simply keep pressing the right cursor key until the COLUMN is wide enough to display Fred's full entry. When you are satisfied that everything looks OK, press ↵.

## Printing

Printing can clearly only occur when you have access to a printer (!), and both it and your software will have to be properly set up to work together. A general appendix such as this can not possibly detail such specifics, thus we will assume that a correctly set up printer is available. If it is not, simply read through this section and then skip to the next.

[L] To print your spreadsheet, press **/** to activate the menu, then **P** for Print. Now select **P** for Printer and **R** to set the Range of cells you wish to print. Move the CELL POINTER to cell **A1**, press the full stop key to lock on to this cell, move to cell **C9**, and press ↵ Now press **G** for Go. After a brief pause, a hardcopy of your work should start to appear on your printer. Press the 'escape' key (Esc – on the top left of your keyboard) four times to get back to the worksheet.

## *Creating a graph*

Spreadsheet programs offer a wide range of graphics display facilities for data presentation. We will now create a bar graph from the data in our spreadsheet.

[M]  Move to cell **B4**. Activate the menu and type **G** for Graph. First we will select the Type of graph we wish to display, so press **T** for Type, and then **B** to select a Bar graph. Now you need to set the graph's data ranges. The *x*-axis of your graph will list our drinking buddies, so press **X** for X range. With the cell pointer located on **B4**, press the full-stop key to lock the cursor, and move to **B7** to block in all the names (**B4..B7**), before pressing ↵. Now set the A data range to the tabs data, by selecting **A** and setting this range to **C4..C7** Pressing **V** for View will now display your graph – which should look something like figure A.2.

## *Adding titles*

[N]  Press the 'Esc' key to bring you back to the graph menu. You can now define some titles for you graph (as in figure A.2) by selecting **O** for Options and **T** for Titles. Next select **F** for First title, and enter **BAR TABS** (or any other title you consider appropriate). Then select Titles again, **Y** for y-axis and enter a title such as **Tab Value (£)** to display alongside the horizontal axis. Press **Q** to Quit from the Options menu, and then select **V** again to view your graph. Finally, press **esc**ape several times to return back to the worksheet.

## *Note!*

As a general rule, pressing the 'Esc' key a number of times will usually get you back to the worksheet if you get in trouble – for example if you accidentally activate a command menu that you do wish to access.

# BAR TABS

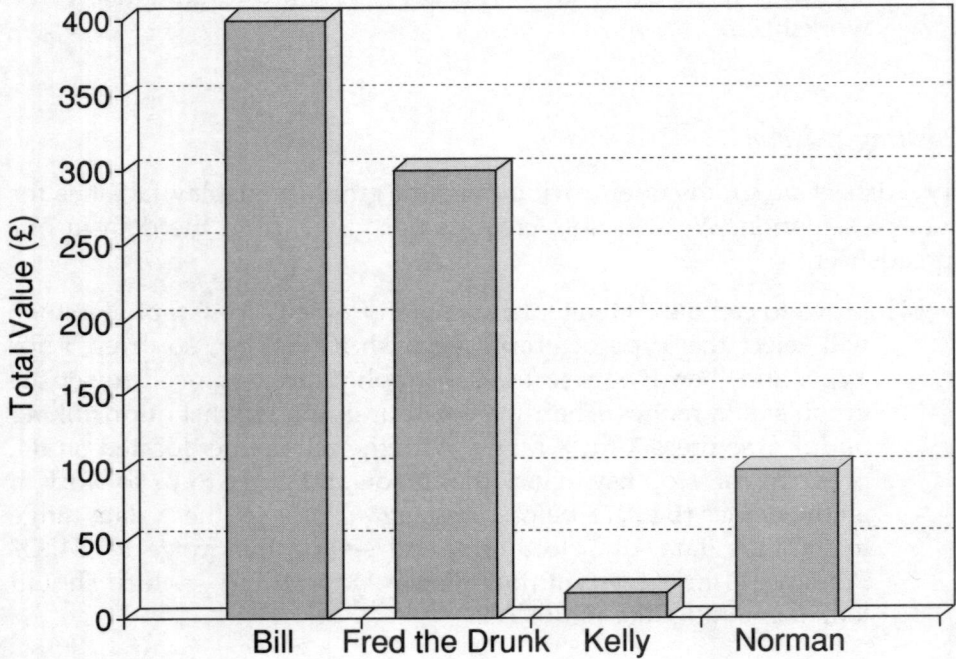

**Figure A.2**   Exercise 1: bar tabs graph

## Saving your work

As with printing, saving work to disk depends to some extent on how your software is set up, and what options are available to you. We will assume, however, that you will be saving your work on a floppy disk, which will be inserted in the **a:** drive of your PC. We will also assume that you have a formatted floppy disk available at this stage!

[O] Before commencing file operations (such as saving or loading worksheets) insert your floppy disc into the **a:** drive of your computer. Then press / to activate the menu, **F** for file, and **D** for directory. If you find that your spreadsheet is already set to access your floppy drive (i.e. **a:** is displayed as the default entry), simply press ↵. If **a:** is not displayed, and instead the default reads something like **c:\123**, edit the entry so that it reads **a:** and press ↵. Your floppy disk will spin, with its activity indicator briefly illuminating. The spreadsheet is now set to access your floppy drive.

[P] To save your spreadsheet model press **/** to activate the menu, then **F** for File and **S** for Save. Then type a filename of no more than eight letters, with no spaces (for example **CHEERS**) and press ↵. Your work will be saved on your floppy disk.

*Quattro Pro* **users only!!!** When saving you may get a message stating that your file contains information that won't translate, with the question 'Save the File?' This is perfectly normal in *Quattro Pro* in *Lotus 1-2-3* mode. Simply answer **Y** for Yes.

[Q] To make sure that your file is saved, activate the menu, type **F** for File, **L** for List, and **W** for Worksheet – all the files on your disk will be displayed on screen. Press **esc**ape five times to return to the worksheet.

[R] To erase your work from the computer, activate the menu and type **W** for Worksheet, **E** for Erase and **Y** for Yes, to confirm your selection. Your worksheet is cleared.

[S] To retrieve your file, activate the menu and type **F** for File and **R** for Retrieve. The file name you used may already be highlighted (if not, move the cursor block so it is), and press ↵. Your work is restored!

## Finally

[T] Select **Q**uit and **Y**es to leave the spreadsheet. (You may at this point be presented with still further messages asking if you really want to quit – simply answer that you do.)

You have now survived your first spreadsheet session! A full 'solution' to exercise 1 appears at the end of this appendix.

## Exercise 2

### Replicating formula

This exercise primarily introduces the spreadsheet COPY command, and the slightly complex notion of *absolute* and *relative* cell addresses. These are first explained via a simple example, before a more complex model is created.

*The test marks*

[A]  Firstly, enter the information contained in figure A.3 into a new worksheet.

[B]  The figures in the 'Mark' column are marks out of fifty for students Mickey, Henry and Sledge. A percentage mark will thus obtained by multiplying these marks by 2. Thus, into cell **C3** enter the formula **+B3*2**.

*The COPY function*

Rather than having to enter individual formula into cells **C4** and **C5**, we can COPY the formula that already exists in cell **C3**.

[C]  Firstly, move to cell **C3** (i.e. the cell you wish to COPY FROM). Next activate the menu (via **/**), and press **C** for COPY. The range to copy **FROM** is just **C3** (displayed at the top of the screen as **C3..C3**), so simply press ↵ to select this. You are now asked for the range to copy **TO**, so move the cursor to **C4** (whose reference is now displayed at the top of the screen). Because you want to highlight more than just one cell, lock the cursor onto cell **C4** by pressing the fullstop key. Note that **C4..C4** now appears at the top of the screen (rather than simply **C4**). Move the cursor to **C5** (hence range **C4..C5**

|   | A | B | C | D |
|---|---|---|---|---|
| 1 |   |   |   |   |
| 2 |   | Mark | Percent | Final |
| 3 | Mickey | 10 |   |   |
| 4 | Henry | 25 |   |   |
| 5 | Sledge | 40 |   |   |
| 6 |   |   |   |   |
| 7 | Fiddle | 10 |   |   |
| 8 |   |   |   |   |

**Figure A.3**  Exercise 2: test mark spreadsheet

is displayed), and press ↵. The COPY is complete: the figures 50 and 80 should appear in cells **C4** and **C5** respectively.

Move the cell pointer to look at the formula that has been created in **C4** and **C5** (the contents of the cell at the present cell pointer location are always displayed at the top left of your screen). You will note that the program has automatically adjusted them in a *relative* manner: i.e. **C4** contains +B4*2, whereas the formula you copied (from **C3**) was +B3*2. This has happened because the 'B3' part of the formula was a *relative* cell address: i.e. it will alter in a relative fashion when copied. Most of the time this is very useful for replicating similar formula – but not always. . .

## *The fiddle factor!*

[D]   Suppose, for example, it has been decided that the final marks are all too low and must be fiddled! A fiddle factor of 10 per cent is to be added to all marks (this figure being a potential variable, and thus being stored in a separate cell of the worksheet, in this case cell **B7**). Into **D3** you can thus enter the formula, +C3+B7, to obtain the correct answer of 30. Now copy the formula from **D3** to **D4..D5** (following the procedure as in part [C]). The results (50 and 80) that appear in cells **D4** and **D5** will be incorrect! The program has entered +C4+B8 into cell **D4**, not +C4+B7, as desired. Oh dear. . .

[E]   To allow the formula to copy properly, the contents of **D3** must be edited in anticipation of the copy function being used upon them. Thus, instead of holding +C3+B7, cell **D3** should contain the formula +C3+$B$7. The '$' signs before the column and row references of **B7** indicate that this is a *fixed* cell address, and must not be altered when copying. Make this change to **D3**, and then again copy the contents of **D3** to **D4..D5**. The correct answers (60 and 90) should result (with the program entering +C4+$B$7 into **D4**, and +C5+$B$7 into **D5**.)

This may well sound confusing (and rather pointless!) at first, but knowing how to copy formula, and in particular how to specify relative and absolute address, is perhaps the most important thing to learn about spreadsheets. Once you are happy with the above example, you can attack the far more complex (and business related!) one that follows.

## A break even model for 'Cough-Not' production

'Cough-Not' is a new wonder drug to sooth the throats other cough mixtures cannot reach. The monthly costs involved in its production (from treacle and aspirin) appear in figure A.4. The cost of the treacle and aspirin used per month clearly depends on the number of batches of Cough-Not made, hence their cost is *variable*. Rent on the plant, electricity usage and wages, however, are *fixed costs* that must be paid each month regardless of the level of output. Batches of Cough-Not are expected to retail for £250.

[A]  Enter the information concerning Cough-Not production in figure A.4 into a new worksheet. The exact cells into which you choose to enter the data are clearly optional, but to stay in sync with the following you may wish to enter 'FIXED COSTS PER MONTH' into **B2**, 'Plant Rental' into **B4**, 'VAR COSTS PER BATCH' into **F2**, and

| FIXED COSTS PER MONTH | | VAR COSTS PER BATCH | |
|---|---|---|---|
| Plant Rental | £2,500 | Treacle | £20 |
| Electricity | £150 | Aspirin | £10 |
| Wages | £5,000 | | |
| | | | |
| TOTAL FC | | TOTAL VC | |
| | | | |
| RETAIL PRICE | £250 | | |

| QUANTITY | FC | VC | TC | REV | PROFIT |
|---|---|---|---|---|---|
| 10 | | | | | |
| 20 | | | | | |
| 30 | | | | | |
| 40 | | | | | |
| 50 | | | | | |

**Figure A.4**  Exercise 2: break-even data for 'cough-Not' production

so on. The 'TOTAL FC' and 'TOTAL CV' labels will thus be entered into **B8** and **F8**, with the 'RETAIL PRICE' label in **B10**, 'Quantity' in **B12**, and the number 10 in cell **B14**. Remember that you must enter the figures WITHOUT the '£' signs or any commas, and then Format them (within the **Range** menu) to display as Currency, with the appropriate number of decimal places.

## Note!

You may discover that, after being formatted, some figures apparently 'disappear' – to be replaced by a row of '********'s. Do not be alarmed! This simply means that the numbers are too big to display in full with the number of decimal places required. You thus need to re-Format the numbers with fewer decimal places (the Fixed Costs figures requiring no decimal places, for example), or increase the column width. You will *not* have to re-enter the figures.

[B] Enter **@SUM** formulas to calculate the **Total FC** and **Total VC** into cells **D8** and **G8** respectively.

You now need to create formulas to calculate the fixed cost (FC), variable cost (VC), total cost (TC), REVenue and PROFIT figures for each of the quantities of production from 10 to 50. These must be based upon cell references, so that if the current values for FIXED COSTS PER MONTH and VARiable COSTS PER BATCH alter, the formulas you have created will change accordingly.

[C] To begin with, the fixed cost for each quantity produced will clearly always be the same, being the value (7650) that should now be displayed in cell **D8**. Thus, into **C14** you *could* enter **+D8**. You *will*, however, wish to COPY this formula across the entire Quantity range, so instead should enter **+$D$8** into cell **C14**. This will make the reference to D8 *absolute*. and thus it will not change when copied. Make this entry into **C14**, then (with the CELL POINTER) still on this cell, activate the menu and select **C** for COPY. You are then asked for the cell to copy from, which is simply **C14**, so just press ↵. You then need the range to COPY TO, so move to cell **C15**, press the full-stop key to lock the pointer onto this cell, and move to cell **C18**. This will block in the range **C15..C18**, after which you can simply press ↵.

You should now find the figure 7650 is displayed as the FC value for all quantities, with the entry **+$D$8** existing in all cells in this range. You *could*, of course, simply have entered these figures directly, but if you had (or have!) done so, they will not be dependent on the values in cells above, and thus will not lead to a useful working model . . .

[D]  Format the values now displaying in the FC column as Currency.

[E]  You now need values in the VC column. The Variable Cost per quantity produced is calculated simply by multiplying the TOTAL VC per batch by the Quantity value. Thus, into cell **D14** you *could* enter **+B14\*G8**. Remember, however, than this will make both elements of the formula *relative* for COPYing purposes. You thus *need* to enter **+B14\*$G$8** into cell **D14** – the resulting value being 300.

[F]  As previously, COPY the entry in cell **D14** across the whole quantity range (i.e. across **D15..D18**). The resulting VC/Quantity values should be 600, 900, 1200 and 1500.

[G]  Next comes Total Cost. For each quantity value, this will be the summation of the FC and VC figures, so the formula to enter into **E14** is **+C14+D14**. In this case you wish both value to be *relative*, so the entry is OK without any added '$' signs. The value now displayed in **E14** should be 7950.

[H]  Use the COPY command to create the values across the rest of the TC range (**E15..E18**).

[I]  Finally, we come to the REVenue and PROFIT columns. REVenue will simply be Quantity multiplied by the RETAIL PRICE, with the Quantity cell reference *relative* (so that it changes when copied), and the RETAIL PRICE reference *fixed*. The formula for **F14** is thus **+B14\*$D$10**. As previously, copy this formula over the Quantity range below it. The resulting REV values should be 2500, 5000, 7500, 10000 and 12500. The PROFIT column will show REVenue minus Total Cost. The formula for **G14** is thus **+F14-E14** – with no '$' signs, and can be copied over the final Quantity range producing values of −5450, −3250, −1050, 1150 and 3350. Note that the spreadsheet may display the negative figures in brackets, just as accountants do on balance sheets.

[J]  Format all the figures in the grid you have created to be Currency.

The break-even model is now complete, with the actual break-even production value clearly lying between 30 and 40 batches of output (as a loss of 1050 is made with a Quantity value of 30, and a profit of 1150 with

40 units). You can thus plot a break-even point graph to determined the exact Quantity value at which no loss is made.

[K]   Activate the menu, select Graph, and set the Type to Line. Then set the X-axis range to the **Quantity** range (by selecting **X**, moving to the first quantity cell **(B14)**, pressing the full stop, moving to the last quantity figure **(B18)**, and pressing ↵). Similarly set the **A** data range to the **TC** data **(E14..E18)**, and the **B** data range to the REVenue figures **(F14..F18)**. Finally, select View, and a graph (similar to figure A.5) is displayed – indicating a break-even point at about 35 batches of output per month.

The break-even point where your TC and REVenue lines cross is, of course, totally dependent on the cost and retail price figures within your

## Break-Even Graph for 'Cough-Not'

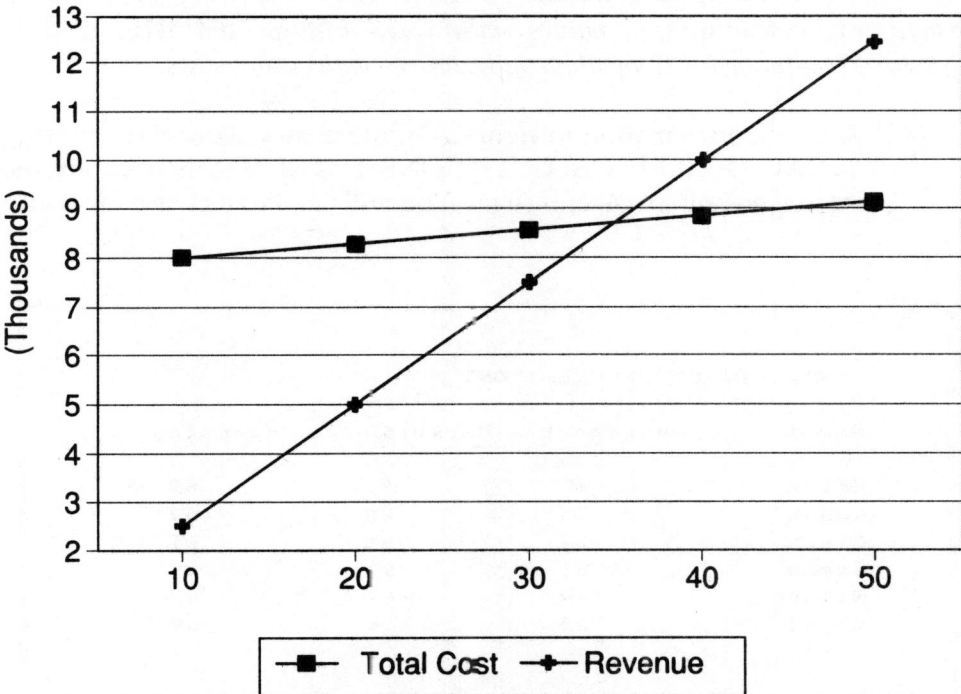

**Figure A.5**   Exercise 2: break-even graph for 'Cough-Not'

spreadsheet. Try **esc**aping back to the worksheet, changing a value (e.g. the Plant Rental to 1500), getting back into the **G**raph menu, and **V**iew-ing the graph again. The break-even point will have changed!

[L]   Finally, within the **G**raph menu, by selecting **O**ptions, you can use the **T**itles option to add a title to your graph, and the and **L**egends option to add data legends to the **A** (Total Cost) and **B** (Revenue) data ranges respectively, so that you graph is easier to read (and more closely resembles that in figure A.5.)

[M]   If you wish (!), save this worksheet (via **F**iles and **S**ave) for future reference.

## Exercise 3

*Exploring @ functions*

*The following example introduces more spreadsheet @ functions, specifically **@AVG, @MAX** and **@MIN**, used to identify the average, maximum and minimum values within cell ranges, and **@IF**, used to produce results based upon the conditions of logic statements.*

[A]   Enter the information in figure A.6 into a new worksheet, placing 'FINAL DEGREE CALCULATIONS in cell **B2**, 'Name:' in **B4**, 'Management' in **C4**, and so on. You will need to increase the width

```
FINAL DEGREE CALCULATIONS

Name:       Management   Marketing  Accounting

Smith           43           71         69
Jones           75           29         52
Brown           34           54         47
Green           81           91         89
Wilson          49           64         81
Scott           23           56         38
```

**Figure A.6**   Exercise 3: student attainment data

of columns **C**, **D** and **E** to accommodate the 'Management', 'Marketing' and 'Accounting' labels.

We will now add some additional information for the examiners, indicating the average, maximum and minimum marks obtained across each of the three subjects taken.

[B] Enter the labels 'MAX', 'MIN' and 'AVERAGE' into cells **B13**, **B15** and **B17** respectively.

[C] To isolate the maximum mark in the Management exam, the **@MAX** function may be utilised. Thus, into cell **C13** enter the formula **@MAX(C6..C11)** ↵. The resulting value should be 81.

Note that most @ functions work by simply typing '@', the function name (in this case MAX for maximum), and then specifying a cell range in brackets (in this case **C6..C4**). Hence:

[D] Enter **@MIN(C6..C11)** as the formula in **C15**, and **@AVG(C6..C11)** into **C17**. Once this is done, you can simply COPY your MAX, MIN and AVERAGE formulas across to the Marketing and Accounting columns, as in previous examples.

[E] Use the **Range Format Fixed** option to format the AVERAGE marks to display with one decimal place – the resulting AVERAGE figures should be 50.8, 60.8 and 62.7 for the three subjects in turn.

[F] Plot a bar graph of the subject average marks. Within the **Graph** menu, simply set the **Type** to **Bar**, the **X** range to **C4..E4** (i.e. the subject names), and the **A** data range to **C17..E17**. With the addition of a title, your masterpiece should then **View** similar to figure A.7.

So far we have produced additional information for the examiners on a subject basis. Average marks per student across their three subjects would also be useful, however, as would automatic recommendations on their final award . . .

[G] Enter the label 'Average' in **F4** and the formula **@AVG(C6..E6)** in cell **F6**. Then copy this formula over the rest of the student range (i.e. **F7..F11**). Once formatted to one decimal place, the resulting values should be 61.0, 52.0, 45.0, 87.0, 64.7 and 39.0

## *Awarding student grades*

The examiners are going to award grades to students, based upon their overall averages, as follows:

# Subject Average Marks (%)

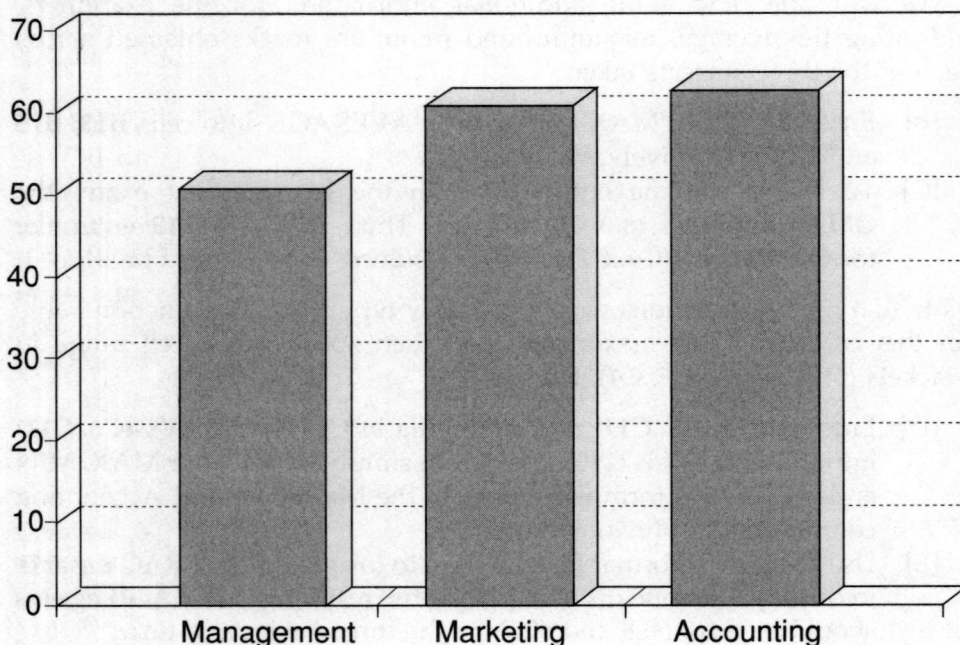

**Figure A.7**   Exercise 3: subject average marks

| | |
|---|---|
| below 40 | Fail |
| 40–69 | Pass |
| 70+ | Distinction |

A column may thus be added to your spreadsheet to display these values, though to automate the process the *principle* of the **@IF** function first needs to be introduced.

## The @IF function

The formula **@IF(cond, x, y)**, when entered into a cell, returns the value *x* if 'cond' is TRUE, or the value *y* if 'cond' is FALSE. 'Cond' must be a numeric value or a formula; *x* and *y* can be either numbers, cell references or text. For example:

$$@IF(B3-C3>0,B3-C3,0)$$

returns **B3-C3** when **B3-C3** is positive (i.e. greater than 0), otherwise it returns a value of zero.

@IF functions can also be *nested* to handle more than two logical conditions at the same time. For example:

**@IF(A1<5,1000,@IF(A1<10,2000,3000))**

will return 1000 if **A1** is less than 5, 2000 if **A1** is greater than or equal to 5 but less than 10, and finally 3000 if **A1** is greater than or equal to 10.)

When @IF statements are nested, you always require one less @IF than the number of conditions to isolate: i.e. one @IF for two conditions (true or false), two @IFs for three conditions, and so on. This may at first appear confusing, unless you have a logical mind, though should become clearer as we progress with the example. We will first simply create an @IF formula that distinguishes whether students have failed or passed based upon their average mark.

[H]  Enter the label 'AWARD' into cell **G4**.

[I]  Into **G6** then enter the formula **@IF(F6<40,"Fail","Pass")**

The result should be the word 'Pass' displaying in cell **G6**, because Smith's mark is not less than 40. Note that 'Fail' and 'Pass' in the **@IF** statement must be entered within quotation marks, because they are items of text, rather than numbers.

[J]  COPY the formula from **G6** over the rest of the range (i.e. **G7..G11**): all student should record a 'Pass' mark, except for poor old Scott, who receives a 'Fail'.

So far so good – students who have passed have been distinguished from those who failed. But what about the distinction awards? To isolate these, you need to 'nest' a second **@IF** statement within the first, to check for the pass marks that are also 70 or over.

[K]  Alter the formula in **G6** to read **@IF(F6<40,"Fail"**, **@IF(F6<70, "Pass","Distinction"))** Then COPY this formula over the range below (**G7..G11**). The resulting Awards should be Pass, Pass, Pass, Distinction, Pass, Fail.

Look at the **@IF** statement you have now entered. It is, in fact, quite simple. Firstly, it checks to see if the value in the **F** column is less than 40. If this is the case (i.e. the statement is true), then the first given result, 'Fail', is selected, and the second **@IF** statement ignored. If, however, the **F** value is not less than 40 (i.e. the statement is false), then the second **@IF** statement is encountered. If this turns out to be true (i.e. the **F** value is less than 70), then the first result of this statement is chosen, namely 'Pass'. Finally, if the second statement is false, 'Distinction' is selected as the result to display. Also note that because two **@IF** statements have been 'opened', two brackets are required to close them both at the end of the formula.

[L] Save this worksheet for future reference – and for use in exercise 4, which follows.

## Other useful @ functions

A host of @ functions are available in most *Lotus 1-2-3* compatible spreadsheet packages. Of particular significance if you have an interest in statistics are the following:

@COUNT(range)    returns the number of numeric cells in the range;
@STD(range)      returns the standard deviation of a range of cells; and finally
@VAR(range)      returns the variance of a population.

## Exercise 4

### Sorting spreadsheet data

As a tail-end exercise to this introduction to spreadsheet operations – which will hopefully lead you on to much greater things! – the **Data Sort** function of the spreadsheet will be examined. Various **Data** functions exist within *Lotus 1-2-3* compatible spreadsheets, allowing tables of data to be manipulated. The **Sort** function is probably one of the most useful, however, as well as the easiest to operate. We will use the 'FINAL DEGREE CALCULATIONS' spreadsheet already created to illustrate its function – so either load this back from disk, or simply continue from where exercise 3 left off.

Firstly, we will first sort all the student data alphabetically.

[A] Activate the command menu and select **Data** and **Sort**. You first have to set the whole **Data Range** to be worked upon, which needs to be all the student information. Hence press **D** for **Data Range**, move to cell **B6**, lock the cursor to this cell with the fullstop key, and move to **G11** to block in the whole range **B6..G11**, and press ↵. Next you must select the **Primary Key** for data sorting – i.e. the category of data to govern the sorting operation. As we are sorting by name alphabetically, select the **Primary Key** option and set the range to **B6..B11** ↵. You will then be prompted for a sort order (A or D). When sorting text entries (as here), select **A** for Alphabetic. (If you were sorting numerical entries, you would select either **A** for Ascending, or **D** for Descending).

[B]  Both the **Data Range** and the **Primary Key** should now be set, so select **Go** to perform the sort operation.

Hey presto! All the student mark and award data is rearranged – in the order Brown, Green, Jones, Scott, Smith and Wilson. We will now sort the data by the Average mark column.

[C]  Activate the menu and select **Data** and **Sort**. You do *not* have to reset the **Date Range** (unless you wish to work on a different block of data!), so only the **Primary Key** needs to be altered. Hence select **Primary Key**, press **escape** to clear the 'old' block, move the cursor to the first average mark (i.e. **F6**), lock it with the full-stop, and block in **F6..F11**. Press ↵ and select **D** for a descending sort order. Finally press **G** for **Go**.

The student information should now be sorted by their Average marks – the order being Green, Wilson, Smith, Jones, Brown and finally Scott. If you like, repeat operation [C] above but specify an Ascending sort order: the students now appearing in reverse order, by Average.

## Using multiple sort keys

If you wish, you can sort data by more than one criteria. This is more significant for larger tables of data than for that in our example (six records is hardly a great number!), though we can at least demonstrate the principle here, sorting the data by Award class alphabetically, and also alphabetically by student name.

[D]  Within the **Data Sort** menu, set the **Primary Key** to **G6..G11**, and then the **Secondary Key** to **B6..B11**. Select **G** for **Go**.

The data should now be arranged listing Green (Distinction), Scott (Fail), and then the Pass students alphabetically (Brown, Jones, Smith and Wilson). This particular sort is perhaps not very meaningful given the data within our example, but does at least demonstrate the use of multiple keys. Finally, note that the entire allocation of **Data Sort** settings may be cleared via the **Reset** option.

## Summary

The above exercises have hopefully demonstrated the basic form of spreadsheet operation, indicating the nature of business tasks to which they may be applied. Specifically, you should now be familiar with the following:

- Entering text labels, numbers and formula based upon cell references.
- Formatting numerical entries (e.g. to display as currency, or to a specific number of decimal places).
- Changing the width of spreadsheet columns.
- Producing graphs from worksheet data.
- Copying formulas, and the role of absolute and relative cell addresses in copy operations.
- The operation of @ functions, in particular @SUM, @AVG, @MIN and @MAX.
- The use of the @IF logical function, and the nesting of @IF statements.
- Sorting tables of data, both alphabetically and numerically, by single or multiple criteria.

You are now encouraged to experiment further with your spreadsheet. Once familiar with their basic rules of operation (such as the use of the command menu, and the blocking of ranges within commands), most spreadsheet functions are fairly clear in their operation, and a great deal can be learnt through experimentation. Indeed, I personally believe that experimentation provides the only path to enlightened software under-standing – the learning process being driven by user need. Finally, sample 'solutions' for the above exercises (full worksheet views, together with the key formula behind them) now follow. Also personally recommended are the following texts, which (in addition to software publisher's manuals), may aid readers in their further exploration of business spreadsheet applications.

## Texts for further study

Diacogiannis, G. and De Souza, E. 1991: *Lotus 1-2-3 for Finance and Business.* Reading, Mass.: Addison-Wesley.

Taylor, G. 1991: *Lotus 1-2-3 Training Guide.* London: Pitman (a similar guide is also available specifically for *Quattro Pro*).

Herzlich, P. *Illustrated Lotus 1-2-3.* London: David Fulton.

## Sample 'solutions''

*Exercise 1*

See figure A.8. The only formula used here is **@SUM(C4..C7)** in cell **C9**.

*Exercise 2*

See figure A.9. Key formula are follows:

| | |
|-----|-------------------|
| **D8** | **@SUM(D4..D6)** |
| **G8** | **@SUM(G4..G5)** |
| **C14** | **+$D$8** |
| **D14** | **+B14*$G$8** |
| **E14** | **+C14+D14** |
| **F14** | **+B14*$D$10** |
| **G14** | **+F14-E14** |

Formulas in the block **C15..G18** should all have been copied from the first row of formula in cells **C14..G14**, whose contents are listed above.

| | A | B | C | D |
|-----|---|---|---|---|
| 1 | | | | |
| 2 | | BAR TABS | | |
| 3 | | | | |
| 4 | | Bill | £400.00 | |
| 5 | | Fred the Drunk | £300.00 | |
| 6 | | Kelly | £17.23 | |
| 7 | | Norman | £98.00 | |
| 8 | | | | |
| 9 | | TOTAL | £815.23 | |
| 10 | | | | |

**Figure A.8**  Exercise 1: 'solution'

|  | A | B | C | D | E | F | G | H |
|---|---|---|---|---|---|---|---|---|
| 1 |  |  |  |  |  |  |  |  |
| 2 |  | FIXED COSTS PER MONTH |  |  |  | VAR COSTS PER BATCH |  |  |
| 3 |  |  |  |  |  |  |  |  |
| 4 |  | Plant Rental |  | £2,500 |  | Treacle | £20 |  |
| 5 |  | Electricity |  | £150 |  | Asprin | £10 |  |
| 6 |  | Wages |  | £5,000 |  |  |  |  |
| 7 |  |  |  |  |  |  |  |  |
| 8 |  | TOTAL FC |  | £7,650 |  | TOTAL VC | £30 |  |
| 9 |  |  |  |  |  |  |  |  |
| 10 |  | RETAIL PRICE |  | £250 |  |  |  |  |
| 11 |  |  |  |  |  |  |  |  |
| 12 |  | Quantity | FC | VC | TC | REV | PROFIT |  |
| 13 |  |  |  |  |  |  |  |  |
| 14 |  | 10 | £7,650 | £300 | £7,950 | £2,500 | (£5,450) |  |
| 15 |  | 20 | £7,650 | £600 | £8,250 | £5,000 | (£3,250) |  |
| 16 |  | 30 | £7,650 | £900 | £8,550 | £7,500 | (£1,050) |  |
| 17 |  | 40 | £7,650 | £1,200 | £8,850 | £10,000 | £1,150 |  |
| 18 |  | 50 | £7,650 | £1,500 | £9,150 | £12,500 | £3,350 |  |
| 19 |  |  |  |  |  |  |  |  |

**Figure A.9** Exercise 2: 'solution'

|  | A | B | C | D | E | F | G |
|---|---|---|---|---|---|---|---|
| 1 |  |  |  |  |  |  |  |
| 2 |  | FINAL DEGREE CALCULATIONS |  |  |  |  |  |
| 3 |  |  |  |  |  |  |  |
| 4 |  | Name: | Management | Marketing | Accounting | Average | Award |
| 5 |  |  |  |  |  |  |  |
| 6 |  | Smith | 43 | 71 | 69 | 61.0 | Pass |
| 7 |  | Jones | 75 | 29 | 52 | 52.0 | Pass |
| 8 |  | Brown | 34 | 54 | 47 | 45.0 | Pass |
| 9 |  | Green | 81 | 91 | 89 | 87.0 | Distinction |
| 10 |  | Wilson | 49 | 64 | 81 | 64.7 | Pass |
| 11 |  | Scott | 23 | 56 | 38 | 39.0 | Fail |
| 12 |  |  |  |  |  |  |  |
| 13 |  | MAX | 81 | 91 | 89 |  |  |
| 14 |  |  |  |  |  |  |  |
| 15 |  | MIN | 23 | 29 | 38 |  |  |
| 16 |  |  |  |  |  |  |  |
| 17 |  | AVERAG | 50.8 | 60.8 | 62.7 |  |  |
| 18 |  |  |  |  |  |  |  |
| 19 |  |  |  |  |  |  |  |

**Figure A.10** Exercise 3: 'solution'

*Exercise 3*

See figure A.10. Key formulas here, from which others should have been copied (either downwards or sideways) to produce the full spreadsheet, are:

| | |
|---|---|
| F6 | @AVG(C6..E6) |
| G6 | @IF(F6<40,"Fail",@IF(F6<70,"Pass","Distinction")) |
| C13 | @MAX(C6..C11) |
| C15 | @MIN(C6..C11) |
| C17 | @AVG(C6..C11) |

# Glossary

**286**  80286: the CPU in some older IBM PC or compatible computers.

**386**  80306: until recently the most common CPU in IBM PC and compatible computers. Much faster than the 286 microprocessor.

**486**  80486: now the standard CPU in most new IBM PC or compatible computers. Faster than the 80386.

**AI**  Artificial intelligence. The synthesis of cognitive processes into computing machines.

**Amiga**  Non-IBM compatible personal computer range from Commodore frequently used for DTV work.

**Apple Macintosh**<sup>TM</sup>  Non-IBM compatible personal computer range with an easy to use graphical interface. Popular for DTP.

**Applications packages**  See software.

**Atari ST/TT**  Non-IBM compatible personal computer range often used by musicians to control instruments electronically via its built-in Musical Instrument Digital Interface port.

**Augmentation**  The process of assisting (rather than automating) non-routine, creative and one-of-a-kind activities.

**Automation**  The use of technology to accomplish routine, repetitive, non-creative work processes.

**Batch processing**  Where data is processed at intervals once batches of transactions have been compiled. For example, banks update customer account balances overnight in one batch rather than continuously and interactively throughout the day.

**Binary code**  The most basic form of computer data. Binary code represents all items via a stream of numerical digits '1' and '0', paralleling to electronic switches within the computer being either 'on' or 'off'. Of significance only to programmers, business users will never need to work with binary code.

**Biometric**  A characteristic unique to an individual that may be verified as a means of identification. Increasingly important in designing computer security systems, common biometrics include fingerprints, retinal patterns and signatures.

**Bug**  A mistake in the specification or coding of a computer program leading to operational errors.

**Bulletin board**   A network facility that users may access to both post and read electronic messages.

**Byte**   One character of computer storage

**CAD**   Computer-aided design. A software genre allowing users to draft complex drawings or models.

**CD-I**   Compact Disk Interactive. A multimedia system developed by Phillips.

**CD-ROM**   An optical disk, physically identical to an audio compact disk, on which computer databases and multimedia applications may be supplied. Users cannot store their own data on CD-ROM.

**CLI**   Command line interface. A form of user interface where the user must enter specific keyboard commands.

**Client–server architecture**   Where many small 'client' computers are provided with services, such as common applications programs or shared data, by a central, complimentary 'server' computer.

**Coaxial cabling**   A form of high-quality network wiring that can carry data over relatively long distances across LANs.

**Computer Misuse Act (1990)**   UK legislation providing a means of prosecution of those who gain unauthorized access to a computer system or who corrupt its data or operations.

**CPU**   Central processing unit. The silicon chip that manipulates data within the computer. The 'heart' of the machine.

**CRT monitor**   A form of computer display using a cathode ray tube as used in television sets.

**Cursor**   The block on a computer screen indicating where user entry will appear.

**Cyberphobia**   A medical condition resulting from technostress where those who fear or mistrust computers suffer physical symptoms such as nausea and high blood pressure.

**Cyberspace**   The virtual medium of computers in which software operates. Also created when computers are linked across networks, cyberspace is the electronic domain of pure information.

**Daisywheel printer**   A type of slow, high-quality printer that cannot produce graphics.

**Data**   The raw material of information. Held on computers in a digital form, data comes in a variety of formats. For example, text, numbers, images and sounds are all forms of data.

**Data media**   The physical hardware on which computer software and data are stored. The most common example is a floppy disk.

**Data Protection Act (1984)**   UK legislation to protect the rights of people on whom information is held in computer systems.

**Data Protection Registrar**   The UK Government officer with whom most information databases must be registered under the Data Protection Act.

**Database**   A file containing a collection of computer records. Database programs allow the manipulation and storage of information for purposes such as payroll, accounts and stock control.

**Dataglove**   An input device allowing humans to interact with computer-created 'cyberworlds' within virtual reality simulations.

**Datastream**   A database service accessed over a network providing subscribers with company financial information.

**Digitizer**   Any hardware device that captures data into a computer. A video digitizer captures pictures from a camera or VCR. A sound digitizer converts audio data into a computer form.

**Directive 90/270/EEC**   Legislation introduced by the European Health and Safety Directive which specifies minimum working conditions relating to those who 'habitually work with display screen equipment' within the EC.

**Directory**   A user-created subdivision upon a computer disk analogous to one drawer in a filing cabinet. Directories are created to allow organized data storage and efficient file management.

**DOS**   See MS-DOS®.

**Dot matrix printer**   An output device that forms letters and graphics by striking small pins against a fabric ribbon to create a pattern of dots on the paper.

**Downsizing**   Referring to the increasing trend of employing small computers and local area networks instead of larger mini and mainframe computers connected to dumb terminals.

**DP**   Data processing. DP information systems may be used to automate routine, repetitive work such as the processing of accounts.

**DSS**   Decision support system. A form of management information system with additional program modules added to enable managers to run 'what-if?' analysis to aid their decision making.

**DTP**   Desktop publishing. DTP programs allow the user total freedom in the layout of text and graphics within their documents.

**DTV**   Desktop video. Using a computer to assist in video production.

**Dumb terminal**   A screen and console device with no internal processing power. Dumb terminals are used to communicate with mainframe and minicomputers

**Dynamic network structure**   An organizational form in which a central 'core' coordinates the activities of several marketplace agents.

**E-mail**   Electronic mail. A means of sending messages between computer users.

**EIS**   Executive information system. A highly interactive information system used by top executives to survey organizational operations and highlight potential problem areas.

**Ergonomics**   The study of people in relation to their work environment, and the design and manipulation of that environment for comfort, safety and efficiency.

**Ethernet**   A common type of local area network, using coaxial cabling as the connection link between computers.

**Expert system**   A specialist form of artificial intelligence embodying a knowledge of a narrow field into a computer system for purposes of prediction and diagnosis.

**FDDI**   Fibre distributed data interface. An item of network hardware used for computer communications over optical glass fibres.

**File management** Operations carried out to keep the information stored in a computer systematically organized.

**Flash RAM** The data storage media used on many small computers and electronic organizers. Data can only be erased from Flash RAM in bulk via exposure to a flash of UV light from a tube within the computer.

**Floppy disk** The most common form of data media. Floppy disks are available in two common sizes, $3\frac{1}{2}''$ and $5\frac{1}{4}''$, and store data magnetically on a thin disk within a square plastic housing.

**Floptical disk** A new development in optical storage. Current floptical disks are the same physical size as $35\frac{1}{2}''$ floppy disks, but with over ten times the storage capacity.

**Flowchart** A pictorial representation of data processing and information flows.

**Formatting** The process that initializes a disk so that it can store information.

**Genlock** An item of hardware to combine live video and computer graphics.

**Graphics tablet** An input device that codes information upon its drawing surface into computer data.

**GUI** Graphical user interface. A form of user interface employing icons to represent files and data, and a pointer to highlight options and commands.

**Hacker** One who gains unauthorized access to a computer system, frequently over the telephone network.

**Hard disk** A high-capacity storage device found resident inside most PCs. The hard disk usually contains a computer's operating system, applications programs and some user data files.

**Hardcopy** Printed computer output.

**Hardware** All the physical components of a computer system.

**HCI** Human–computer interaction. The discipline concerned with the interface of humans and computers, and hence the design and development of user interfaces.

**Hot-site agreement** An arrangement with a supplier wherein if a disaster befalls a client's computer a compatible back-up system will be made available.

**IBM PC** See PC.

**IBM** International Business Machines. The inventors of the IBM PC.

**Icon** Small pictorial representation of a computer program or data file within a WIMP environment.

**Information** Data that has been processed into a useful form and hence has some value to the user.

**Ink-jet printer** Also in a form known as 'bubblejet'. These printers spray ink onto the paper to create high-quality text and graphics output.

**Integrated package** A software suite combining the functions of other packages. Most integrated packages include a word processor, spreadsheet and database program.

**IS** Information system. A combination of work practices, people and computer technology used to assist organizational performance.

**ISDN**   Integrated Services Digital Network. A high-speed telecommunications link for audio, video and data communications.

**IT**   Information technology. A common term for computer and communications systems hardware. IT will comprise one element of an IS.

**Justification**   Referring to the method used to align text between a document's margins.

**Kilobyte**   1024 bytes of computer storage. Usually abbreviated to 'Kb'.

**LAN**   Local area network. Means of interconnecting PCs for data communications and program resource sharing over relatively small distances.

**Landmark speed**   An indication of how fast software will run on one computer in comparison to others. The higher the landmark figure, the faster the computer.

**Laser printer**   Fast, high-quality output device using xerox technology to output computer text and graphics one page at a time.

**LCD**   Liquid crystal display. Flat, low-power form of computer display hardware, as used on most portable computers. Twisted crystal and retardation film technologies are now improving the quality of LCD screens, and colour displays are also now available.

**Logic bomb**   A malicious computer program that resides dormant in a computer system until triggered by an particular event or instruction. It then wreaks havoc with computer data and operations.

**Magneto-optical disk**   A high-capacity, high-speed storage device on which data is written and read by optical means but erased magnetically.

**Mailmerge**   The word processor function allowing a personalized standard letter to be automatically compiled from a master document and a database of names and addresses.

**Mainframe**   A very large computer, usually accessed via a dumb terminal.

**Maths co-processor**   A silicon chip that may be fitted to a PC to improve the speed of programs dependent upon a large number of mathematical calculations. The maths co-processor eases the strain on the main CPU, in effect doing all of its 'hard sums'!

**Megabyte**   1024 kilobytes of computer storage, i.e. 1Mb = 1024Kb.

**MICR**   Magnetic ink character reader. Computer input device commonly used to read the digits on cheques.

**Microcomputer**   See personal computer.

**Microprocessor**   See CPU.

**Microsoft® Windows™**   The graphical user interface or WIMP environment common on IBM PC and compatible computers.

**Minicomputer**   Variant of computer hardware smaller than a mainframe but larger than a personal computer.

**MIS**   Management information system. A DP system which has been programmed to provide additional control or decision information for management purposes.

**Modem**   An item of communications hardware enabling computers to communicate over conventional telephone lines.

**Mouse**  An input device used to move the cursor or pointer around the computer screen.

**MS-DOS**®  Microsoft Disk Operating System. The operating system used on IBM PC and compatible computers. Also known simply as DOS, or sometimes PC-DOS.

**Multi-factor security**  A computer system possesses multi-factor security when a user must identify themselves by more than one means of authentication. Identification factors may be chosen from a password, a token (such as a credit card), and a biometric.

**Multimedia**  The integration of computer-generated text, graphics and sound, and usually involving CD-ROM data storage.

**Network**  Any means of connecting several computers to share data or program resources.

**Newton**  The range of PDAs from Apple Computer.

**OAS**  Office automation system. Any computer application used to aid information processing within the office. Examples include word processing and electronic mail systems.

**Operating system**  A form of low-level program that coordinates operations such as disk storage, keyboard input and printer control, and thus permits the operation of higher-level applications packages.

**Outsourcing**  Putting organizational functions out to tender in the marketplace.

**PC**  Personal computer. A small desktop computer, usually comprising a separate display screen, mouse and keyboard. Most PCs are either produced by IBM, or are compatible 'clones' of IBM PCs and hence will run the same software programs. The term 'PC' is often used to refer to any IBM or compatible PC.

**PCMCIA**  Personal Computer Memory Card International Association. PCMCIA cards are a credit-card sized media for data storage.

**PD**  Public domain. PD software is created for pleasure by enthusiasts and may be freely copied and distributed.

**PDA**  Personal digital assistant. This new, small and powerful breed of computers-cum-communications-devices are operated by writing and drawing with a pen on their display screen.

**Peer-to-Peer Network**  A form of small-scale computer network with no server to coordinate activities. All computers on the network are therefore of equal status.

**Pentium**  The latest CPU chip from Intel. Successor to the 80486 microprocessor, the Pentium is the fastest CPU that may be found in IBM PC or compatible computers. Effectively the '80586'.

**Peripheral hardware**  All additional hardware connected to a computer, e.g. the keyboard, mouse or printer.

**Pixel**  One small rectangle on a computer screen. Computer images are built up from thousands of pixels, a typical screen being composed of a matrix 640 pixels wide by 400 pixels high.

**Plotter**  An output device that produces accurate hardcopy by moving a pen over a piece of paper. Common in CAD.

**Pointer**   The small on-screen arrow moved around to activate functions within a WIMP environment.

**PSS**   Packet switched stream. Local PSS nodes are accessed by users to allow them to engage in low-cost national and international computer communications.

**RAM**   Random access memory. The memory within a computer used to store programs and data. The contents of RAM are 'volatile' – in other words they are lost when the computer is turned off.

**Relational database**   A database program with the ability to link different database files. For example, a database storing stock records may be linked to another storing supplier names and addresses.

**RSI**   Repetitive strain injury. A medical condition that may result from excessive computer keyboard operations.

**Sans-serif font**   A typeface without flourishes at its letter stems. One example is Helvetica.

**Scanner**   An item of hardware that allows two-dimensional images to be captured into a computer.

**Serif font**   A typeface with flourishes at its letter stems. Examples include Times and Dutch Roman.

**Server**   A large computer that provides facilities to other machines on a network.

**Shareware**   A try-before-you-buy form of software which is freely distributed. A registration fee becomes payable if a user finds the software useful.

**Smartcard**   A credit card containing computer chips and memory. Increasingly used for a variety of purposes from data storage to user identification.

**Software**   Computer programs. Software is required to bring computer hardware into meaningful operation.

**Spreadsheet**   A form of applications package offering the user an electronic table of columns and rows which may be used to present and manipulate numerical data.

**Subdirectory**   A directory within a directory.

**Supercomputer**   The most powerful type of computer available. Unlikely to be encountered by most business users!

**Surge protector**   An item of hardware that protects computer equipment from failures due to fluctuations in mains power.

**Systems integrators**   Specialists in combining hardware and software, perhaps from many different manufacturers, to form working computer systems.

**Systems development lifecycle**   A common multi-phase methodology detailing the stages to be employed in developing and implementing a new computer system.

**Tape streamer**   The storage device used to back-up computer data to tape cartridges in case of disaster.

**Technostress**   A physical and emotional burnout brought about by an inability to cope with new technology.

**Terminal**   See dumb terminal.

**Token Ring**™ An example of a local area network with computers wired in an unbroken circle.

**Trackball** A device used to move the pointer around a computer screen via rotating a hemisphere atop the unit. Effectively an 'upside-down mouse'.

**Transputer** In essence an entire computer on a single chip. Machines using transputers require less intercomponent wiring, and hence run very quickly.

**Trojan** A malicious program that tempts a user to activate it, after which it spreads throughout computer networks, often wreaking havoc.

**Turing test** A famous benchmark, devised by Alan Turing, against which to measure success in the achievement of artificial intelligence.

**Twisted pair** A form of network cabling used for short-distance computer interconnection.

**User interface** The means used to access a computer. Examples include a CLI or a GUI.

**Users** People who use computers!

**VDU** Visual display unit. The computer screen.

**Virtual reality** An artificial environment created with the computer medium of cyberspace. The ultimate in graphical user interfaces.

**Virus** A maliciously created computer program that corrupts data or program operations. Viruses are usually passed around on 'infected' floppy disks.

**VLF ionizing radiation** A band of electrical emission that emanates from CRT screens and which some experts link to skin sores, rashes, cancer and miscarriages. Exposure may be greatly curtailed by fitting an appropriate filter to the VDU.

**WAN** Wide area network. Any means of communications link allowing computers to communicate over long distances.

**What-if? analysis** The use of a computer model to determine hyperthetical outcomes via the alteration of key dependent variables within the model. For example, what will our profit margin be if interest rates rise to 10%?

**WIMP environment** A form of user interface using windows, icons, menus and pointers for graphical computer instruction. The most common example is *Microsoft*® Windows™'. See also GUI.

**Windows** See *Microsoft*® *Windows*™.

**Wire-pair** See twisted pair.

**Word processing** The use of computers for the layout and manipulation of text.

**Word wrapping** The process by which words typed into a word processor automatically 'wrap' to the next line rather than becoming split at the edge of the page.

**Worm (virus)** A malicious program that takes up residence in a computer's memory, reproduces and often causes the system to crash.

**WORM drive** An optical disk storage media to which data can be written once but read many times.

# Further reading

Although a full list of the references utilized in this *Blueprint* follows, these texts are particularly recommended should readers wish to delve further into the subject of computers in business. None are incredibly technical, and should be accessible to all those who have survived to the end of this book!

Alter, S. L. 1992: *Information Systems: a management perspective.* Reading, Mass.: Addison-Wesley.

Capron, H. L. and Perron, J. D. 1993: *Computers and Information Systems: tools for an information age*, 3rd edn. Redwood City, Calif.: Benjamin/Cummings.

Martin, C. and Powell, P. 1992: *Information Systems: a management perspective.* Maidenhead: McGraw-Hill.

Preece, J. 1993: *A Guide to Usability: human factors in computing.* Wokingham: Addison-Wesley.

Rochester, J. B. and Rochester, R. 1991: *Computers for People: concepts and applications.* Homewood, Ill.: Irwin.

Trimmer, D. 1993: *Downsizing: strategies for success in the modern computer world.*Wokingham: Addison-Wesley.

In addition to the above, readers interested in the future of both business computing and the new modes and structures of organization that may result from their application will find the following stimulating mental fodder:

Davidow, W. H. and Malone, M. S. 1992: *The Virtual Corporation.* New York: Harper Business.

Hayman, S. 1993: *The Electronic Frontier*, transcript adaptation of BBC TV *Horizon* documentary. London: BSS.

Stock, S. 1993: *Metaman: humans, machines, and the birth of a global superorganism*. New York: Bantam Press.

# References

Adriaans, W. 1993: Winning support for your information strategy. *Long Range Planning*, 26(1).

Alter, S. L. 1980: *Decision Support Systems*. Reading, Mass.: Addison-Wesley.

Alter, S. L. 1992: *Information Systems: a management perspective*. Reading, Mass.: Addison-Wesley.

Bainbridge, D. I. 1990: *Computers and the Law*. London: Pitman.

Barnatt, C. J. 1992: The quadrant theory of project management. *OMEGA – The International Journal of Management Science*, 20(4).

Barnatt, C. J. 1993: A prelude to the cyber business. School of Management and Finance discussion paper 1993.XIII, University of Nottingham, UK.

Bertalanffy L. von 1951: Problems of general systems theory: a new approach to the unity of science. *Human Biology*, 23(4).

Bird, J. 1993a: Boom time for the systems integrators. *Management Today*, May 1993.

Bird, J. 1993b: Enter the singing, dancing desktop. *Management Today*, March 1993.

Buck-Lew, M., Pliskin, N. Shaked, I. and Wardle, C. 1992: corporate aquisitions in the 1990s: paying attention to information technology. *Journal of General Management*, 18(2).

*Business Update* 1993: A more natural way of working. Issue 7 (Digital Equipment Co. Ltd).

Callahan, R. E. and Fleenor, P. C. 1987: There are ways to overcome resistance to computers. *Office*, no. 106 (October).

Capron, H. L. and Perron, J. D. 1993: *Computers and Information Systems: tools for an information age*, 3rd edn. Redwood City, Calif.: Benjamin/Cummings.

Clifton, H. D. 1986: *Business Data Systems*, 3rd edn. Englewood Cliffs, NJ: Prentice Hall.

Clough, B. and Mungo, P. 1992: *Approaching Zero: data crime and the computer underworld*. London: Faber & Faber.

Cooley, M. 1987: 'Computers and the mechanization of intellectual work. Reproduced in Morgan, G. 1988: *Creative Organizational Theory: a resource book*. Newbury Park: Sage.

*Computer Shopper* 1993: Newsfile, no. 65 (July).

Daniell, M. 1990: Webs we weave. *Management Today* (February).

Davidow, W. H. and Malone, M. S. 1992: *The Virtual Corporation*. New York: Harper Business.

Dobson, P. and Starkey, K. 1993: *The Strategic Management Blueprint*. Oxford: Blackwell Publishers.

Doyle, E. 1992: Along the right lines. *Personal Computer World*, 15(8).

Eade, C. 1992: Are you sitting comfortably? *Personal Computer World*, 15(12).

Edwards, C., Ward, J. and Bytheway, A. 1991: *The Essence of Information Systems*. Hemel Hempstead: Prentice Hall.

Eilon, S. 1993: Measuring quality of information systems. *OMEGA – The International Journal of Management Science*, 21(2).

Fayol, H. 1949: *General and Industrial Management*. London: Pitman. Translated by Storrs, C. from the original *Administration Industrielle et Generale* (1916).

Gibson, W. 1984: *Neuromancer*. London: Grafton.

Goodwins, R. 1991: Multimedia development kit. *Personal Computer World*, 14(10).

Goodwins, R. 1992: Low-cost LANs. *PC Magazine*, 1(9).

Handy, C. 1993: *Understanding Organizations*, 4th edn. London: Penguin Business.

Hanson, D. 1982: *The New Alchemists*. Boston, Mass.: Little, Brown & Co.

Hayman, S. 1993: *The Electronic Frontier*, transcript adaptation of BBC TV *Horizon* documentary. London: BSS.

Heller, R. 1990: *Culture Shock: the office revolution*. London: Hodder & Stoughton.

IBM 1987: *DOS 3.30 User's Guide*, IBM Corporation and Microsoft Inc.

Jefferson, D. 1993: Visual effects on *Terminator 2*. *Animator*, no. 30.

King, M. and Bone, A. 1989: *Information and Word Processing*. Cheltenham: Stanley Thomas.

Lambert, R. 1993: Implementing computer systems. *Business Studies*, 5(4).

Larson, R. W. and Zimney, D. J. 1990: *The White Collar Shuffle: who does what in today's computerized workplace*. New York: acacom.

Mandell, M. 1991: Corporate computers: how necessary? *Across the Board*, XXVIII3 March 1991.

Martin, C. and Powell, P. 1992: *Information Systems: a management perspective*. Maidenhead: McGraw-Hill.

Martinsons, M. G. 1993: Outsourcing information systems: a strategic partnership with risks. *Long Range Planning*, 26(3).

Mason, J. 1993: RSI ruling casts doubt on future claims for damages. *Financial Times*, 29 October 1993.

Mintzberg, H. 1973: *The Nature of Managerial Work*. New York: Harper & Row.

Mintzberg, H. 1975: The manager's job: folklore and fact. In D. S. Pugh (ed.) 1990: *Organization Theory – selected readings*. London: Penguin Business.

Morgan, G. 1989: *Creative Organization Theory: a resourcebook*. Newbury Park: Sage.

MSA, 1990: Excellence and the IT factor: information technology inside excellent companies in Britain. *Journal of Information Technology*, 5(1).

Parker, D.B. 1976: *Computer Abuse Perpetrators and Vulnerability of Computer Systems*. Proceedings of the Computer Security Conference, Amsterdam.

Porter, M. 1985: Technology and competitive advantage. *Journal of Business Studies* (Winter).

Preece, J. 1993: *A Guide to Usability: human factors in computing*. Wokingham: Addison-Wesley.

Pruitt, S. and Barrett, T. 1991: Corporate virtual workspace. In M. Benedikt (ed.), *Cyberspace: first steps*. Cambridge, Mass.: MIT Press.

Roberts, D. J. 1992: A disaster recovery plan for Nottinghamshire County Council Department of Construction and Design. Dissertation presented in part consideration for the degree of Master of Business Administration, University of Nottingham.

Rochester, J. B. and Rochester, R. 1991: *Computers for People: concepts and applications*. Homewood, Ill.: Irwin.

Rockman, S. 1990: The perils of Emma (hacking and the Computer Misuse Act). *Personal Computer World*, 13(9).

Ross, P. W., Haiduk, H. P, Means, H. W. and Sloger, R. R. 1992: *Understanding Computer Information Systems*. St Paul: West Publishing.

Senker, J. and Senker, P. 1992: Gaining competitive advantage from information technology. *Journal of General Management*, 17(3).

Simson, E. M. von 1990: The 'centrally decentralised' IS organization. *Harvard Business Review*, 86(4).

Stock, S. 1993: *Metaman: humans, machines, and the birth of a global superorganism*. New York: Bantam Press.

Strategic Planning Society 1992: Spreadsheets can't be trusted . . . *Strategic Planning Society News*(October).

Taylor, F. W. 1947: *Scientific Management*. New York: Harper & Row.

Timm, P. R., Peterson, B. D. and Stevens, J. C. 1990: *People at Work: human relations in organizations*, 3rd edn. St Paul: West Publishing.

Trimmer, D. 1993: *Downsizing: strategies for success in the modern computer world*. Wokingham: Addison-Wesley.

Weiss, K. 1992: Controlling the threat to computer security, *Global Management 1992*, Management Centre Europe.

Wood, S. 1992: Is your PC killing you? *Computer Buyer* (January).

Wheatley, M. 1993: 'The flight from the mainframe. *Management Today* (June).

Wilson, K. 1993: Upfront – the Apple Newton Messagepad. *What PC?* (September).

Wyles, C. 1992: Put information technology in its place. *Global Management 1992*, Management Centre Europe.

# Index